MW01106840

Parents' Handbook

Parents' Handbook

NLP & Common Sense Guide
for Family Well-Being

Roger Ellerton, PhD, CMC

The information in this book is not intended as a substitute for family, medical, psychological or other counseling. The author and publisher disclaim any responsibility or liability resulting from actions advocated or discussed in this book.

Order this book online at www.trafford.com
or email orders@trafford.com

Most Trafford titles are also available at major online book retailers.

© Copyright 2010 Roger Ellerton.
All rights reserved. No part of this publication may be reproduced, stored in a retrieval system, or transmitted, in any form or by any means, electronic, mechanical, photocopying, recording, or otherwise, without the written prior permission of the author.

Printed in Victoria, BC, Canada.

ISBN: 978-1-4251-4790-7 (sc)
ISBN: 978-1-4251-4791-4 (eb)

Our mission is to efficiently provide the world's finest, most comprehensive book publishing service, enabling every author to experience success. To find out how to publish your book, your way, and have it available worldwide, visit us online at www.trafford.com

Trafford rev. 1/19/10

 www.trafford.com

North America & international
toll-free: 1 888 232 4444 (USA & Canada)
phone: 250 383 6864 ♦ fax: 812 355 4082

Acknowledgments

I WOULD LIKE TO thank all the people I have known over the years, especially my teachers, family members and friends. Although I may not have known it or appreciated it at the time, you have all had an influence and contributed to my learning about life, and you've helped me to discover what is possible.

I wish to acknowledge and express gratitude to my good friends and co-NLP trainers John Sweetnam and Su Thomas from whom I have learned much, both through our conversations and while delivering trainings together. My utmost thanks to Su Thomas, Kim McLeod, Angela Ohlman and Trevor Wilkins – friends and colleagues – who provided timely, thoughtful and instructive feedback on an earlier version of this manuscript. Arlene Prunkl (editing), Fiona Raven (text design) and Martyn Schmoll (cover design) have made this a book of which I'm truly proud.

Thank you to all my clients and those who have attended my seminars. You have said you learned a great deal from me. And I believe that I have learned as much if not more from you. I am sure you will recognize many of your thoughts in this book.

This book would not be possible without the important contributions of John Grinder and Richard Bandler, co-founders of NLP, and those who followed in their footsteps.

A special thank you to my children, Kim, Deanna, Nick and Matt, whom I never see enough of. You are now on your own, creating your own dreams.

To Donna, my partner, who provided me with encouragement and time to write this book, I extend my deepest appreciation.

My parents, William (deceased) and Irene Ellerton have always stood by me, supported me to the best of their abilities and given me the space to choose my own destiny. Although at times, they must have wondered. Thank you, Mom, for your continuing and unflagging support.

Contents

Preface

I AM NOT A child psychologist, social worker, teacher, doctor, guidance counselor, early childhood educator, daycare worker or family therapist. I do not have any of these credentials. If I did, I would undoubtedly think like them and give you similar advice and ideas. Their advice and ideas are useful and available in many books and magazines.

Then what are my credentials? I am the father of four wonderful children, who, as they grew up, challenged me to their full capacity in many different ways. At times I surpassed my expectations as a parent and other times I struggled. Through it all I did the best that I knew, to the best of my ability. Simply put, when you become a parent you are not handed a manual that will answer all your questions or cover all situations. For many, the "manual" you bring to parenting is the one you learned from observing your parents. If you perceived what your parents did as good, you did that. If you were hurt or felt disadvantaged in some way by your parents' actions, you swore to do something different. Exactly what, you didn't know. Then, when pressured by circumstances, not feeling good about yourself or being resentful of your partner, you dragged baggage from your past and manifested those parental behaviors you swore not to repeat.

As well as having learned much about being a parent, for almost twenty years I have been a student and trainer of neuro-linguistic programming (NLP). NLP is about how you communicate with yourself, and based on the results of this, how you engage in conversation with others. NLP is also about modeling people who are excellent at what they do and making these skills and abilities available to other people. I wish I had known about NLP when I first became a parent. In fact, I wish I'd had the opportunity to learn and practice NLP concepts when I first went to school. I'm sure that my experiences growing up would have been that much richer.

Given what I know today and will share with you in this book, I know that as a parent I could have done much better or achieved the same results with a great deal less stress and anguish for everyone involved.

As an NLP trainer, my students have often said to me, "NLP is a great resource for parents." "I wish I had known these ideas when I first became a parent."

"This information will be useful for my children." Yes indeed, NLP is a great resource for both parents and children. And although some NLP books have been written that discuss parenting and how children learn, I am not aware of any as comprehensive as this book.

My intention in writing this book is to provide you and your family members with thoughts, insights and tools that will prove to be useful and will ultimately bring about a desired change in your lives. You will learn:

- How to have meaningful, supportive conversations with your partner and children.
- How to address beliefs or habits that get in the way of being an effective parent.
- How to help your children address beliefs or habits that limit them.
- How to support your children to learn effectively.
- The skills and abilities for the six different parenting roles.

Although not written specifically for adolescents, the material is presented at a level older teens can understand and use. With the aid of their parents, younger teens will also find many concepts in this book useful. They will learn how to:

- Be more resourceful with family members, teachers and friends.
- Improve their schoolwork and relationships.
- Contribute to their well-being and that of their family.

NLP is not a linear subject. It does not lend itself to fit easily into specific chapters. Some of the material might certainly be presented in an earlier chapter and vice-versa. You may find that once you have read the entire book, the material at the beginning of the book becomes richer and more accessible. For those of you using the book as a reference, an index has been provided to meet your needs.

Mastering the concepts and techniques in this book will give you a wide array of usable skills to assist your children in preparing themselves for a productive and enjoyable future. I trust this book will be a valuable resource and I look forward to receiving any observations you may wish to share with me.

Roger Ellerton
Ottawa, Canada

1.

Introduction

> Before I got married I had six theories
> about bringing up children; now I have
> six children, and no theories.
>
> *— John Wilmot*

PARENTING IS NOT an idea, a concept or a belief. It's a process and therefore is neither static nor fixed in time that results in something special being created. Your activities and responsibilities as a parent evolve with your children, taking into account their needs – physical, social, emotional and intellectual – and your ability to be aware of and to meet these needs. As an effective parent, you help your children overcome perceived limitations to do their best and to be a valued member of the family. All the while, you bump up against your own limitations – many of your own making.

Parents' Handbook: NLP & Common Sense Guide for Family Well-Being provides you with tools, techniques and approaches to improve the way you communicate, to be available emotionally and physically and to successfully fulfill the different roles expected of you as a parent. This book draws on an area of personal development called neuro-linguistic programming (NLP). Those who have experienced or know NLP describe it in different ways. For me there are three critical, related aspects:

- Communicating effectively – with yourself and then with someone else. Do your body language, tone of voice, choice of words and energy you exude support you in achieving what you desire?
- Being resourceful in the moment. When you engage in these conversations, do you feel good about yourself, those you are with and the circumstances? Are you resourceful – confident, calm, humorous – both inside and out? Are you able to create an environment where those you are speaking with –

your partner,[1] your children and their teachers – feel resourceful as well? Or does past baggage get in your way?

- Stepping outside the box. We all limit ourselves in some way. The key is to become aware of these self-imposed limitations and then to make a choice as to whether they will continue to limit us.

You are probably already using NLP concepts to some degree. NLP has its roots in real life behavior rather than in theory and research. NLP is about how people are successful at whatever they do; how they choose to enhance their lives so they can achieve their desires. NLP provides ways of helping anyone become more competent at what they do, more in control of their thoughts, feelings and actions, more positive in their life and better able to achieve results.

This book does not pretend to know what is best for you, nor will it tell you how you and your children should live your lives. It provides a toolkit for healthy parenting and it is the manual on parenting you didn't get when your children were born. It's about recognizing you have choices – you are constantly choosing. You have the choice of parenting the way you were parented (and no doubt you have some valuable experiences to draw on) and getting similar results, or you can choose to do something different and augment your parenting skills with new and effective tools and concepts.

1.1 WHO WOULD USE THIS BOOK?

This book can be used by a variety of audiences:

- Parents who are looking for effective ways to communicate with and support both their children or partner.
- Grandparents and others who from time to time fill the role of parent.
- Teachers who wish to connect with their students in a different way and truly make a difference.
- Teens – with their parents' assistance – who desire effective ways to communicate with family members, friends and teachers, and who are looking for new ways to learn.
- Coaches and those in the helping professions. The concepts and ideas presented in this book are easily transferable to any situation where two or more people interact.
- NLP practitioners who are looking to augment their toolkit.

The ideas in this book are sound. They work if you choose to use and apply them consistently.

---

1. Partner will refer to anyone who interacts with your children in a parenting role, for example, a spouse, biological parent not living under the same roof, adoptive parent, etc.

1.2 GETTING THE MOST OUT OF THIS BOOK

The material has been grouped into eight chapters, each with a particular focus. Due to the non-linear nature of NLP, this is not the only way to group the material. To satisfy a particular need, you may want to make notes and, upon completion of the book, review material from some of the earlier chapters. I strongly recommend marking up the book with your notes in the margins as inspiration strikes you. When you've finished, it will be that much easier to return to passages you found of particular significance.

The NLP self-discovery exercises can be done by you, or you can lead your adolescent children through them. I've found that it's often more fun and the person engaging in the exercise gets better results if someone shares their journey by coaching them through the exercises. A coach helps the participant stay focused and honest. Their participation can range from reading the instructions and offering encouragement to using rapport, questioning, reframing – basic concepts that are presented later in this book.

I have included the words "common sense" in the subtitle, because often after I've explained an NLP concept or technique, people remark, "But isn't that just common sense?" Yes, it is, yet until these ideas are brought to your attention, they are outside of your conscious awareness and not always accessible to you.

The concepts in this book are applicable in all areas of your life, not just in your role as parent. You are limited only by your imagination in your desire to help your children and choose the life you want to live.

To get the most out of this book, I encourage you to:

- Have an outcome in mind for reading this book, other than to simply read it. The Law of Attraction tells us to focus on what we want in life. What do you want for yourself, your children? Take a few moments to write down at least one outcome to focus on as you read this book.
- As you read each section, find at least one idea or technique you can put into action immediately that will make a positive difference in how you parent and the results you achieve.
- Be prepared to refocus your outcome(s). As you read further in this book, your thoughts about parenting and your children may begin to change, resulting in a need to adjust or establish a completely new outcome.
- As you read this book, imagine placing any mental baggage you've been dragging around, perhaps for years, outside with the trash. You know, the stuff that gets in the way of being the parent you really want to be. Concurrently, you may also wish to clean up and remove unnecessary clutter and baggage in your home or in your children's rooms. Often how you outwardly

live your life (e.g., a messy room) is a metaphor for what is going on inside of you. Cleaning up one can positively impact the other.

- Be curious as you read this book. When you come across a new idea, ask yourself: How can I use this? Can this be modified to make it more useful in my situation?

- Accept that NLP is a very useful model for understanding human dynamics and change, and that a model is a generalization about some aspect of the world. No model is 100 percent correct. The question is not whether the model is correct; rather, the question is: Does the model produce useful results? The answer with regard to NLP is a clear, resounding, "Yes, it does!" As you read this book, you can focus – negatively – on finding the few places where the model may not work, or you can accept the general principles and move forward to being the parent your children need.

This book can be equally useful for your older children. They will benefit from understanding how humans communicate, how to put themselves into a resourceful state and how to speak to others, including their parents, with rapport and respect. Even the chapter on the different parental roles can be useful for your children. They can happily reverse roles and "coach" you in terms of learning to communicate the support they need to be healthy and achieve their desires.

1.3 SOME IDEAS AS YOU PREPARE TO READ THE *PARENTS' HANDBOOK*

- Your thoughts and actions in the present create your future.

  Just by reading this introduction your thought processes will have been shifted, even if only slightly, which may result in a different conversation and subsequent actions in the coming days.

  And what if you were to access additional resources that allow you to feel good about yourself and your parenting skills, and to change your thoughts about how you parent – thoughts that allow you to see your children or partner in a more positive light and as a result interact with them differently? Would this not create a new and different future for you and them?

  If you live your life searching for excellence, you will find excellence. If you live your life searching for problems, you will find problems. While none of us are perfect, we can choose to focus on the positives. Where do you choose to focus your thoughts?

- There is the story of a traveler who knocks on the door of a house and, while talking with the inhabitants, notices that their dog is sitting in the corner of the yard howling in pain.

"What's the matter with your dog?" the man asks.

"Oh, he's sitting on a nail," reply the inhabitants.

"Why doesn't he just move?" asks the man in disbelief.

"I guess it doesn't hurt enough," is the reply.

What small hurts do you have within yourself or your family? They may be hurts you complain (howl) about to others, yet you hesitate to take action that will address the situation.

As you well know, if the dog continues to sit on the nail, over time this minor wound will begin to fester, causing a much greater problem. In the longer term this may result in the loss of a limb or even the loss of life.

In the same way, unaddressed issues (wounds) within you or your family may in the longer term result in loss of intimacy with your family, losing touch with a dear family member or, in the extreme, the breakup (loss) of the family. If you're open to it, this book will assist you in addressing your wounds and becoming an effective and loving parent.

If it is to be, it is up to me.

– Anonymous

2.

Understanding the Basics

2.1 WHAT IS NLP?

Its origin

The term *NLP* stands for *neuro-linguistic programming* and was coined in the early seventies by John Grinder, an assistant professor of linguistics at the University of California, Santa Cruz, and Richard Bandler, a student of psychology at the university. They began their work by studying Fritz Perls, a psychotherapist and originator of the Gestalt school of therapy, Virginia Satir, a well-known family therapist and Milton Erickson, a world-famous hypnotherapist. Their intention was to model outstanding therapists and identify patterns in order that other practitioners could use these patterns to generate similar results. Thus, one aspect of NLP is to identify excellence by observing experts, and then devise means for others to use these discoveries to achieve similar results for themselves or with their clients.

> I did not look for "what went wrong"
> or the "whys." I did not look for cures.
> I looked at *what worked*, no matter how.
> – *Richard Bandler, Get the Life You Want,*
> Health Communications Inc., 2008

NLP also draws on earlier scientific discoveries. One of the best-known parts of behavioral learning theory is classical conditioning (stimulus response), which was discovered by Russian physiologist Ivan Pavlov (1904). Classical conditioning is a learning process that occurs through associations between an environmental stimulus and a naturally occurring response. NLP takes theoretical results such as these, notices the practical applications and makes them available to you and me to help us improve our lives and well-being. In NLP, we refer to classical conditioning as *anchoring*.

NLP is more than just techniques. It's a curiosity about how people who are high achievers accomplish what they actually set out to do. It is also a methodology that assists you in discovering those thinking and communication patterns that prevent you from being successful and shows you how to achieve the results of successful people. That is, NLP is a process for discovering experts' patterns of excellence, and making these effective ways of thinking and communicating available for personal benefit or to assist others.

NLP had its origins in modeling outstanding therapists, and today experts in virtually all fields have been modeled for their excellence. The resulting models have found application in all areas of human endeavor – education, health, sports, management, and, perhaps most importantly, interpersonal relations. Indeed, it would be difficult to attend any workshop or training course involving human interaction – sales, alternative dispute resolution, presentation skills, communication, management – that did not contain NLP concepts, although these concepts are often not identified as originating from NLP.

Today, hundreds of thousands of people have studied NLP, incorporating it into their daily lives. Most major cities in the developed world have one or more organizations offering NLP training.

Neuro-linguistic programming

Neuro refers to your neurology – your sense organs: visual (see), auditory (hear), kinesthetic (tactile touch or emotional feeling), gustatory (taste) and olfactory (smell). You experience or perceive events/information via these means.

Linguistic refers to how you use the language of the mind – pictures, sounds, feelings, tastes, smells and words, referred to as internal representations – to remember, represent and make sense of a particular experience or to forecast a future experience. For example, can you recall the last time you sat on the floor and played with your children? When you remember playing with your children, in your mind do you see a picture? What about sounds? And how were you feeling – happy, tired, excited? Add in specific words that represent some form of code (e.g., boring, exciting), and this is how you remember or put language to an event or experience.

Think about a major event in the future. What kinds of pictures, sounds, feelings, tastes and smells come to mind relevant to that event? Do you envision yourself being successful? Or failing? Or is the image nondescript? The pictures, sounds, feelings, tastes, smells and words that you use to describe your future experiences have a bearing on what actually happens. You do create your own reality!

Programming refers to your habits, patterns, programs and strategies – those things you do without really thinking about them. If it's a school day, do you follow a particular routine as you help get your children ready? Perhaps you like to lie in bed an extra five minutes after the alarm goes off. Do you wake your children right away or have a shower first? If you take time to look at what you do, you'll see a pattern that you follow in getting your children ready. If for some reason you don't follow that pattern, do you find yourself feeling that something is missing?

Having a ritual for getting up in the morning or any other regularly performed activity is useful. You do not have to take time each day to rediscover it. For the most part, you run it at an unconscious level, giving your conscious mind time and resources to handle other things (for example, how am I going to make a difference at the parent-teacher meeting this evening?).

Mindlessly (unconsciously) following a habit or program can have unwanted consequences as well, particularly if it is a habit or program that worked well to keep you safe or get what you wanted when you were five years old, and you're still running this program as an adult with a family of your own. Or perhaps you run an automatic pattern (I often refer to it as a dance) with your partner or children – mindlessly going through the same basic behaviors and getting the same boring or unwanted results. If you want different results, you have to change the dance, ritual or habit.

You have patterns, habits, strategies and programs for everything you do. Some of these patterns serve you; others do not – resulting in unwanted outcomes. You may be fully aware of some of your patterns. You may become aware of other patterns only when someone brings them to your attention. And you may choose to quickly forget about these patterns because you want to avoid addressing that part of your life. And there are still other patterns that you are not aware of at all, yet they continue to influence how you look after yourself, communicate with family members and perform your daily tasks. If those patterns you're aware of serve you – that is, generate positive results in your life – great! However, if you find that some patterns do not serve you, would it not be useful to identify those patterns and to change them so they work to your advantage?

To further illustrate these unconscious programs, many of us are fully functioning, capable, decisive adults, until we cross the threshold of our parents' home. Then we revert to those old patterns or habits that we exhibited as a child.

You are the one who chose the programs that run at a conscious or unconscious level. And you are the one who can change them. The first step is to become aware of these programs, and the second step is to replace them with those that can help you to live and achieve what you desire. For me, this is one of the biggest benefits of NLP.

NLP new code

NLP has evolved and continues to evolve ever since Richard Bandler and John Grinder made their first discoveries. One of the more interesting changes is what John Grinder calls NLP New Code.

Originally, NLP focused mainly on consciously manipulating internal representations – adjusting in your mind the picture (e.g., brighter, dimmer), sounds, feelings, tastes and smells to change your perception and hence your behavior. Great results were obtained through these methods, yet often the unconscious mind was not directly engaged. Given that your conscious mind processes seven plus or minus two items at a time whereas your unconscious mind runs your whole body (digesting food, growing hair, healing the wound on your arm), continuously scans the environment for danger or rewards, maintains all of your memories, strategies, beliefs and so on, a major part of the change process was missing.

Realizing this, John Grinder and Judith DeLozier developed NLP new code (*Turtles All the Way Down*, Grinder and Associates, 1987), which also takes a systemic approach, emphasizing relationships between and within systems. Thus, NLP moved from being viewed as a collection of techniques that can simply be applied like a recipe to involving your unconscious mind and often your body responses in effecting long-lasting change.

I have integrated discoveries from both of the NLP models, as each has their advantages and uses.

2.2 HOW YOU PROCESS INFORMATION

The NLP communication model (figure 1) provides interesting insights into how you process information and how this processing has a bearing on your behaviors and what you achieve in life:

- You observe an event with your senses (see, hear, feel, taste and smell).
- You generalize, delete and distort (filter) this information according to what you perceive to be important – according to your beliefs, values, decisions, etc.
- You make internal representations (pictures, sounds, feelings, tastes, smells and code words) based on this filtered information and call this reality. In NLP terms this is referred to as a map.
- These internal representations influence your internal state, which influences your behaviors (external physiology, actions, choice of words and tone of voice).

Changing your filters (beliefs, values, etc.) will affect what you pay attention to and thus how you react to the world around you.

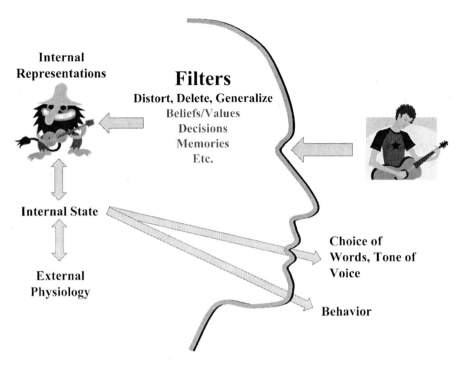

FIGURE I: NLP COMMUNICATION MODEL

The following sections build on this model and add to your understanding.

Conscious awareness

At any given moment, your senses and hence your unconscious mind are exposed to about four billion bits of information. Are you consciously aware of all of this information? Of course not. For example, at this moment are you aware of how your left foot feels? I suspect that until I mentioned it, you were not aware of how your left foot felt, and I'll bet you are aware of it now. Before I drew your attention to your left foot, you didn't perceive the information that was coming to you via your left foot as important – unless you have something wrong with your left foot. Since you did not perceive this information to be important you filtered it out. What other information are you filtering out at this time? Take a moment to hear what sounds are available to you that you were not fully aware of a few moments ago. Or continue looking at your book, and without moving your eyes, perhaps you now become aware of other things you can see.

What's going on here? Of the four billion bits of information available to your unconscious mind, your conscious mind can only process about two thousand bits, or about 0.00005 percent of this information. To consciously process more of this information would either drive you crazy or be such a distraction that you could not function.

What two thousand bits of information does your conscious mind pay attention to? The two thousand bits that it perceives to be important at the time. Before I drew your attention to your left foot, that information was not perceived to be important, yet once I mentioned it, it is perceived to be more important.

Here's an example to further illustrate this point. For burn victims, the treatment for a burn is far worse than the injury. Instead of traditional distraction devices, such as books and music, since 2007 Nationwide Children's Hospital Burn Center (Columbus, Ohio) has been using virtual reality games to distract patients while nurses attend to the patients' burn wounds. As a result, burn nurses report patients are more able to tolerate dressing changes.

You've undoubtedly experienced times when you've been so completely engaged in reading a book, watching TV or working on a hobby that you were unaware of activities going on around you. Yet, if your newborn cried in a certain way or a family member called for help, you suddenly forgot what you were doing and focused your two thousand bits on these new important needs.

Filters – deleting, distorting and generalizing

What happens to all this other information? Your brain filters it from your conscious awareness through:

- *Deleting* is the process of paying attention to information you perceive to be important and deleting the rest. By eliminating extraneous information, you can attend to what you perceive to be important. You may overly focus on one child and not pay sufficient attention to other family members, causing them to act out in some way in order to get the attention they would like.
- *Distorting* is the process of changing the relationship between experiences. Distorting can provide you with a different view of reality, which can lead you to seeing and experiencing the world differently from others. This may open up new possibilities for you, and it may lead to disagreements when your interpretation of reality conflicts with that of others. Simplifying, exaggerating and daydreaming are examples of distorting.
- *Generalizing* is the process of taking one or a limited number of experiences and projecting it to other similar experiences. As a child, if you burned your hand when you touched a hot stove, you generalized or formed a rule not to touch hot stoves. In a similar manner, if you were hurt by your father in a certain situation, you may have generalized this to not engage your father (and perhaps all men) in that way.

What you actually delete, distort and generalize depends on your beliefs about parenting, values (perhaps conflicting values – providing for your family or actually spending time with them), language (the meaning you assign to words), decisions and memories. Let's look at a few examples to gain an appreciation of how they work.

Beliefs and values

If you believe you don't have good parenting skills, what two thousand bits of information are you paying attention to? All those times that you do not meet your expectations, thus reinforcing the belief. On the other hand, if you do believe you have good parenting skills, you are paying attention to the two thousand bits that support this belief and filtering out the rest. In a similar fashion, if you value being successful, this is what you will observe. And the opposite is also true. That is, if you value or are looking for times when you or a family member fails, you will find and focus on this information.

Both types of information are available to you at any given moment. Whichever type you pay attention to reinforces the beliefs/values you already have about yourself or others. What information do you pay attention to (perceive to be important) on a regular basis? And what information are your children paying attention to or filtering out? As a result, are they creating a world that supports who they can truly be or creating a world that keeps them small?

Are the beliefs and values you hold dear the same as those of your partner? If not, you will each observe and interpret your children's behaviors differently, which can lead to arguments between the two of you and confusion for your children.

Decisions

You make decisions (generalizations) about what you are capable of doing ("I'm good at figuring things out" or "mathematics is difficult"), what you enjoy ("sports are fun" or "English class is boring"), the abilities/rights of others ("men should go to work and women should stay home"), etc. These decisions filter how you experience the world around you. Some of these decisions open up all sorts of possibilities, while others severely limit what is possible. Children do not come into this world with these decisions already in place. They adopt the spoken and unspoken decisions of their family, school system and community and create new ones based on their interpretation of events as they grow up. Often, these decisions become sacred rules that are not to be violated, and their validity is seldom challenged. What decisions have you made about yourself, your family or the world in general that limits what is possible for you or your family, while other people are open to new ideas and possibilities?

Filters

Have you ever gone with your child to see a movie, sat next to each other and watched exactly the same movie, yet one of you thought it was the best movie you'd ever seen and the other thought it a waste of time? How could that happen? It's quite simple. You and your child filtered the information differently, employing different beliefs, values and decisions. You each perceived the movie differently; hence, you each reacted differently to it.

An understanding of filters helps to explain why not everyone experiences the world the same way, nor wants the same rewards from life, nor reacts in the same manner to a specific event. This does not make one person right or the other wrong; It's simply that people interpret things differently depending on their filters.

You may find it interesting to examine the origin of your filters. Who put those filters in place? Recall the same person who put your habits, strategies and generalizations in place. Of course, it is you. You chose these filters, based on what happened in your family as you grew up, the teachings of your religion (or the absence of religion), the beliefs and values in the part of the country in which you lived and the decisions you made about the world (for instance, a safe place or a dangerous place). If your filters are not creating the results you desire, you are the only person who can change them. The first step is to become consciously aware of the filters you have created and what kind of reality and results they are returning for you.

Internal representations

Do you remember having breakfast this morning? How do you remember it? Do you see a picture in your mind, or are there smells or tastes? Are there sounds – perhaps in your mind you can hear a radio? To remember an event, your mind uses pictures, sounds, feelings, tastes, smells and words. These perceptions of your "outside world" are called *internal representations* and are a function of your filters. Your perceptions are what you consider to be "real," in other words, your reality.

If you and your partner have breakfast together, your internal representations or perception of the occasion will most likely be similar in some ways and different in others, depending on what is important or unimportant to each of you (your filters). Breakfast is not very controversial. However, what about your respective views on how to raise children? Given your different backgrounds, you may, in each of your minds, see, hear and feel differently about how children should behave and hence exhibit significantly different behaviors with your children.

Internal representations and behaviors

Would you like to see the effect internal representations have on your behaviors? Then fully play along with me and imagine a dill pickle on a plate in front of you. Notice how it looks. And remember the sound of biting into a crisp, juicy dill pickle as the juice flows across your tongue and all around your mouth. And what does that taste like? That's right, take a moment to fully experience the taste of a dill pickle. What I've done is helped you recall certain pictures, sounds, feelings and tastes in your mind. And if you've ever eaten a dill pickle, I suspect you are either salivating right now or reacting in some way to the idea of eating a dill pickle. In either case, I did not ask you to have that physical reaction. You had it in response to the internal representations you made in your mind. This demonstrates that the internal representations you create in your mind influence your physiology. Carrying this further, they influence your choice of words, the tone of voice you use and the behaviors you manifest. In the same way, when you think of a particular family member, you will create a positive, neutral or negative set of internal representations of him[2] that will influence your body language, choice of words, tone of voice and, in general, how you interact with him.

Now for another exercise: Sit up straight, put a big smile on your face, tilt your head up slightly and breathe deeply. While you do that, attempt to feel sad. I am almost certain that you cannot feel sad without changing your physiology (for example, shallow breathing and rounded shoulders). This illustrates that your physiology influences your state – whether you feel sad or happy – which in turn influences your internal representations. Next time you're feeling sad or down, the best antidote is to participate in some physical activity such as a brisk walk or other form of mild exercise.

Another example: Through your filters – what you choose to observe – suppose you interpret a family member's actions to be out of alignment with your beliefs/values. In the blink of an eye, your mind calls up internal representations in the form of pictures, sounds and feelings of previous events that reinforce your assessment of this person (the box you have put him in) – your reality. With these internal representations at the forefront of your mind, what do you think your physiology will be like when you begin to talk to him? What about your tone of voice or the words you use? Given those behaviors, do you think he will fully understand what you are saying and do what you suggest? Most likely not! And what has he done? He's verified your interpretation of reality and proven once more that he is indeed the person you made him out to be.

2.3 FIVE STEPS FOR SUCCESS

Most successful people follow (consciously or unconsciously) five simple steps, some of which may occur concurrently:

1. Have clearly defined and simply described outcomes that you are enthusiastic about achieving.

    As a parent, what outcomes do you have? To simply have children? Undoubtedly, it is much more than that! Choosing to wander through the experience of being a parent is an outcome, yet it's not good enough. What are your desires for yourself, for your children? And what can you accomplish today that will move you further along this path?

2. To avoid the use of "he/she," I have chosen to alternate between using "he" and "she."

If you have not set an outcome for today, your children or partner will most likely enlist you to help them get what they want. And you may (silently or otherwise) become angry at them for taking advantage of you, when in reality you set the stage for what happened. Be conscious of the choices you're making and the consequences or rewards that follow.

2. Take action through persistent steps that move you toward this outcome.

Many people with a clear outcome do not take action to achieve it. How many times have you heard a friend (or even yourself) talk passionately about doing something for their family, yet they never fully commit to it and it remains nothing but a dream, year after year.

3. Pay attention. Use your senses and milestones to observe if you are making acceptable progress or if corrective action is required.

You need to be continually aware of your outcome(s); as well, you need some form of measure to know whether you're making progress. If you don't, how will you know if or when you have actually achieved your outcome(s)?

4. Be flexible in your approach. Notice what is not working and take corrective action to overcome these obstacles.

On occasion, you may find yourself locked into a course of action that you know that is not generating what you desire. However, you've been reluctant to change course for a variety of reasons: you want to avoid admitting you've made a mistake, you're afraid of not knowing the consequences, etc. Yet when you take time to think about it, there are many ways you can be flexible: ask for assistance, take a number of small steps instead of one large step, use the ideas presented later in this book and so on.

> Real difficulties can be overcome; it is only
> the imaginary ones that are unconquerable.
> – *Evan Bailyn*

5. Strive for excellence. Be the best you can be physically and mentally – bring all of your resources into play.

Recall from the NLP communication model that your thoughts (internal representations) affect your physiology and your physiology affects your thoughts. In your mind, have thoughts (pictures, sounds, feelings, tastes and smells) of having achieved your outcome(s), while adopting a supporting physiology – walk, talk, dress as if you have already achieved it.

Taking one, two, three or four of these steps is just not good enough. What use is it to have an outcome if you don't take action? Nor is it useful to take action if you are not paying attention to the results you are creating. How often have you missed achieving something important by not being flexible? And then you wonder why your life is the same today as it was yesterday, last month or last year. And the dreams you have dreamed are still just dreams.

A daily five-step action plan for children and parents

To achieve what you desire, you need to make it a focus of your daily activities. The following is one way to do this. If this is too large of a commitment at this time, do what is reasonable for you. Then gradually increase until you are performing the following five activities each day:

1. At the beginning of each day, decide on a minimum of three activities (no matter how big or small) that you will undertake during the day that are in alignment with your outcome. Plan how, when and with whom you will undertake these activities. Write this down and give a copy to your partner, or if you're guiding your children through this action plan, make sure they write down their activities and give you a copy.
2. Share your planned activities with people who may be able to help you – friends, colleagues, teachers, etc. Networking or sharing your activities with people who care can increase your chances for success.
3. Thank those people who speak negatively about what you plan to achieve and move on to others who are willing to support you.
4. At the end of each day, review what you have achieved with your partner or parents, keeping in mind: "There is no failure only feedback." That is, learn from what did not go as planned.
5. Just before going to bed, identify a short list of possible activities for the next day. Then sleep on it and notice what comes up.

2.4 THE STRUCTURE OF REALITY

What is reality? Why is it that some people see a task or an outcome as possible (within their reality) and others completely discount it?

> Reality is merely an illusion, albeit
> a very persistent one.
>
> *– Albert Einstein*

Your perception of the world is your reality

The NLP communication model illustrates how you filter information based on your beliefs, values and memories. As a result of this filtering, you have a perception of the world that you call reality. There is a saying: "If you wish to change your life, first you must change the way you perceive your life."

To get a better understanding of reality and how it affects you and your children, consider the following: Assume the circle in figure 2 represents all possible knowledge – all that has been discovered and all that remains to be discovered. One piece of this circle represents "what you know you know" – you know your name, where you live and so forth. Another piece of the circle represents "what you know you don't know" – while you know there is something called scuba diving, you do not know any of the details or how to do it. These two pieces represent what you call reality (or your perception of reality). The rest of the circle is "what you don't know you don't know" and is, at this time, outside of your perception (reality). Because it is not part of your awareness or reality doesn't mean that it does not have an effect on your life. For example, until I tell you, are you aware that you have a new stomach lining every five days? (Deepak Chopra, *Perfect Health: The Complete Mind/Body Guide*, 2000.)

There is a fourth part to the circle – "what you don't know you know." This can have many interpretations. For example, some adults have painful memories from childhood that they have chosen to suppress. Or children may be culturally conditioned to take on certain roles and not others – boys are to follow in the footsteps of their fathers. For simplicity, I have chosen to include this as part of "what you don't know you don't know."

Stepping into the unknown

If you were to step out of your reality to do something you've never done before with no idea of how it might turn out, how might you feel? Fearful, apprehensive or confused are some words that come to mind. And it doesn't have to be a big step to generate some of these feelings. For example, I remember the birth of my first child. I had never looked after a baby before. I thought I was prepared. Yet, on her first day at home, she cried when my wife was not available, surprising my dog who started barking, which made her cry even more, and I did not have the help of the hospital nursing staff whom I had relied on previously. At that time, I have to admit that I was unsure, fearful, confused and let's also throw in anxious for good measure. How about you – have you been in a similar situation? Instead of feeling some of the emotions that I did, your mind may have simply gone blank for a moment. For the arrival of my other children, it was quite different. Looking after a baby was firmly established as part of my reality and I was able to look after them very easily, without any of the previous upsets.

Virginia Satir, a foremost family therapist, believed that the strongest instinct in human beings is to live in "what you know you know" – your comfort zone. This creates an illusion of being safe and comfortable, even if you are not. People are terrified of the unknown – "what you don't know you don't know." Sometimes they actually do harm to themselves or others to avoid experiencing it. Avoiding

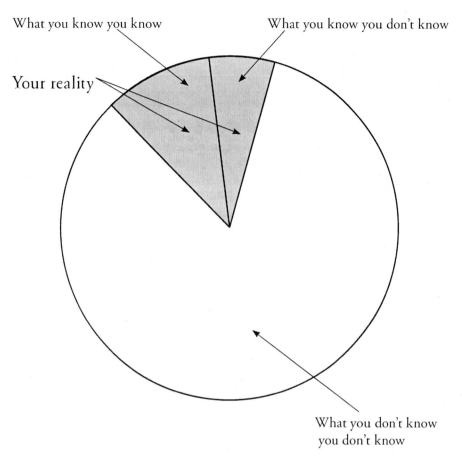

FIGURE 2: YOUR REALITY AND STEPPING OUTSIDE OF IT

the unknown keeps you small. Only by stepping into "what you don't know you don't know" are you able to expand your reality. An expanded reality gives you more choices, more freedom and greater opportunity to enjoy life and be fully supportive of your children.

What is your typical reaction when you face the unknown? Many people rush back to something they know and perceive to be safe – their familiar reality (hand the baby to someone else) – and shut down any process of exploring new ideas about the world, themselves or how to parent their children. If you are to expand your reality and your potential, explore "what you don't know you don't know."

Feeling fearful, confused or having your mind go blank generally indicates you are on the verge of discovering something new. The next time you have any of these feelings of self-doubt, first make sure you are safe, then relax, breathe deeply and venture forth taking one small, reasonable step at a time. You now have the opportunity to discover new insights about who you are, your beliefs and values, your strategies for achieving what you want in life or how you can better manage those everyday situations that caused you problems in the past.

Appreciating your children's reality

With the speed of change in today's society, it is not unusual for your children to be exposed to different ideas, beliefs/values, and challenges than those you confronted at their age. It would not be surprising to find that a great deal of their reality falls into your "what you don't know you don't know" zone, resulting in very different perceptions of the world. What is the potential for each of you to agree and work together as a family unit? If you both hold fast to your beliefs/values, and are not willing to explore new ideas, you will undoubtedly be continually disagreeing. On the other hand, what would happen if you decide to explore your children's reality? You needn't agree with them, only appreciate and respect that they can have different beliefs/values from yours and avoid judging which of your belief/value systems is right or wrong. At first you may find their reality confusing. However, if you are flexible and continue to explore their reality with them, you have the potential to expand your own awareness (bring more choices into your life), assist them in being more tolerant of your reality and open up the possibility to improve your communication with one another.

Real change comes from exploring "what you don't know you don't know"

Finally, let's talk briefly about real change – change in how you interact with others and what you achieve in life. Referring to figure 2, think about where the innovative real change will occur. Will it be found in doing what you have done in the past (what you know you know)? Most decidedly not. From "what you know you don't know"? In this case, there is some potential for small advances. Or will the innovative ideas come from stepping into "what you don't know you don't know." Yes – here, ultimately, is where the opportunity lies for big breakthroughs.

NLP tools and techniques can assist you in expanding your reality – stepping into the unknown in a safe, resourceful and respectful way. Once you are able to do this for yourself or with the aid of someone else, you will have the knowledge and experience to assist members of your family to do so as well.

2.5 GUIDING PRINCIPLES FOR PARENTS

The foundation for NLP is a set of presuppositions (beliefs) about ourselves and the world we live in. These presuppositions also serve as principles to guide how we live our lives or function as parents. Depending on the author, the number of NLP presuppositions and the wording may vary, yet the basic intent is the same. I will not claim that all of these presuppositions are absolutely true in all possible situations. I do believe they are true in the vast majority of situations. You can spend your time trying to find the rare exception to when the presupposition does not hold, or you can acknowledge there may be exceptions and focus on all of the times you can use them to your advantage.

The following are my favorites. You may find some of them are already part of your life. You may also find one or more of them confusing or unrealistic. In this case, they may be part of "what you don't know you don't know." As a result, there may be value for you to step into this belief and explore what you can discover about yourself and what else is possible.

1. **You cannot not communicate.**

   Often we think we communicate only through the words we say or write. This is not so. You also communicate through your tone of voice, body language and actions. You may say the "right" words, and if your tone of voice or body language is not in alignment with those words, which message is really received? Even no communication sends a message, and it is often not a positive one.

   Purchasing a special gift for someone or doing something you know they will like, just because you want to, sends a powerful message. The same is true for not living up to your promises and commitments. Take time to step back and see the impact of your actions on the larger system – your family. Is this really the impression you wish to create or the message you wish to convey?

2. **The map is not the territory.**

   I live in Ottawa, Canada. To get an idea of where places are located in Ottawa, I can refer to a street map. The map is not Ottawa; it is a visual representation. Someone else, with a different purpose in mind, could draw an entirely different representation – for example, a topographical map. Both would represent Ottawa and give a different perspective.

   In a similar way, you remember your experiences by creating maps (internal representations – pictures, sounds, feelings, tastes, smells and words) in your mind of what you perceive to be important – a function of your beliefs, values and decisions (your filters).

   Your memory (map) of an event is not the event. How you choose to represent the map in your mind is what gives meaning to the event for you. If you and your partner attended the same event (perhaps an outing where you interact with your children), each of your maps might be quite different, depending on your filters. Later, when you discuss the event, you may disagree on certain points. You're not really disagreeing on the event itself or what happened at the event. Rather, you have differing interpretations (maps) of the event. In other words, your differences are based on what you perceived, which depends upon your filters. So the real discussion is about your differences in beliefs, values and decisions.

Your senses take in raw data from your environment and that raw data has absolutely no meaning whatsoever other than the meaning or "map" you choose to give it. If you were to choose a different meaning, this would change your experience of that event.

People act and react according to their map of reality, not to reality itself. NLP is about changing these maps – not reality – so you can improve your interactions with others and achieve what you desire as a parent or in other parts of your life.

3. **Respect the other person's model of the world.**
    You have your own unique interpretation of reality – your own view or model of the world – which has a significant unconscious influence on your behaviors. Your interpretation of reality may be quite similar to or differ vastly from another person's.

    We each map our experience of the world differently, because we all have different sets of experiences and filters. You may not understand or agree with my behavior. However, if you had a similar upbringing to mine, you may well have adopted beliefs, values, decisions and interpretations of reality comparable to mine.

    You don't have to agree with the other person's model of the world, only respect that she may see, hear, feel and interpret the world differently than you do. As a result, she may be motivated by different values, make different choices and hence behave differently. It's not personal. She simply has a different perspective of the world.

    The Golden Rule states: "Do unto others as you would have others do unto you." Perhaps the Platinum Rule should state: "Do unto others by respecting their model of the world."

4. **The family member with the most flexibility of behavior will have the most influence.**
    Have you ever been stuck in life, doing the same things repeatedly and each time expecting to get a different result? This is the widely known definition of *insanity*. If you want your life to be different, doing the same things more often, harder or louder is not the way to change it. You must choose to do something different. If you try one key in a lock and it doesn't fit, would

you keep trying the same key repeatedly? Or would you be flexible and try other keys until you find the one that works?

Children are great examples of being flexible enough to influence the system and get what they want. Perhaps they ask one parent, then the other, maybe they will promise to be good (forever!) or perhaps begin to cry or yell and scream. Although some of the behaviors may not be welcomed, this is flexibility! As parents, we do not demonstrate flexibility regularly; instead, we are often seen as rigid in our behaviors and viewpoint. Note that I do not imply in any way that giving into your child's demands is demonstrating flexibility.

Have you ever noticed someone in your family being very inflexible, trying to control everything? He lives under the illusion that he is in charge. In reality, other family members simply find ways to avoid dealing with him. Another member of the family may be someone whom people enjoy talking with and helping. Why? Because by being flexible in her behaviors and knowing her boundaries, she is able to assist others and communicate her needs as required. Others see her as a valuable asset in their lives.

5. **The meaning of communication is the response it produces.**
   Your intended communication is not always what is understood by the other person. It does not matter what your intention is; what matters is how the other person interprets your communication and the results you generate from your words, tone of voice, facial expression and body language. By being flexible, you can change how you communicate until you achieve your desired outcome.

   Consider the following situation. Your child comes home pleased and excited, having received an A-minus on her assignment. You are also very pleased until you notice an error, and to help her improve and do even better next time, you point this out in a caring and supportive manner. She gets upset and runs to her room. Her reaction is not what you expected. Obviously she heard your message very differently from what you had intended. Perhaps, in her model of the world and through her filters, she felt as though you did not see her as "good enough." You can leave it at that and decide she simply needs to grow out of it. Or you can recognize that your comment did not produce the result you had intended and, being flexible, find different ways to communicate with her so that you both enjoy a loving, caring and supporting relationship.

6. **There is no failure, only feedback.**
   You do something and it doesn't work out the way you had planned. How often do you interpret this as failure?

Think of when your children first learned to walk. They would tentatively stand, maybe attempt a step and fall down. Then, they would immediately get up and attempt to walk again. At no time did they view the previous attempt as failure or immediately conclude "Well, I guess I'm just not a walker!" Instead, they took it as an opportunity to learn and see how far they could get next time.

How different would it be for your family if each of you viewed failure simply as *feedback* – an opportunity to learn how *not* to do something and to become flexible in developing new ways to achieve your intended outcomes? Would this give each of you permission and encouragement to undertake new things, be curious and be potentially more successful in life?

> Failure is simply the opportunity to begin again,
> this time more intelligently.
>
> – *Henry Ford*

7. **Everyone does the best they can with the resources available to them.**
   Resources can be interpreted as either physical (e.g., financial, strength) or mental (e.g., feeling confident, safe, powerful). Similar ways to phrase this presupposition are: "This is the best choice available to this person given the circumstances as they see them" or "There are no unresourceful people, only unresourceful states of mind."

In NLP, we believe you, as well as other members of your family, already have the resources (at least the mental ones) you need to succeed. However, your model of the world (with its limiting beliefs and constraints) may restrict you from seeing what is really possible or prevent you from accessing your full capabilities and resources. Or you may be in a temporary state of mind (overwhelmed, sad, angry) that prevents you from fully accessing all of your resources. In these situations, you may make certain decisions or take actions that, from another viewpoint, are much less effective than you are capable of and that may even be experienced as hurtful.

With hindsight or with a larger, more resourceful interpretation of reality, you could have done many things differently. Yet your choice was deemed the best choice at the time. You do not always make the "right" decision or take the "right" action; simply, decisions and actions are based on what resources you have available at the time.

If your mother or father did not know how to love themselves or each other, how would it be possible for them to teach you to love yourself? Your parents were doing the best they could with the understanding, awareness and knowledge they had at that time. They could only teach you what they themselves knew. If they had been raised differently, or had access to resources that helped them to love themselves, they would have been equipped with an expanded model of the world and thus more choice in the behaviors they exhibited and taught.

8. **Every behavior has a positive intention.**
No matter how strange, hurtful or inappropriate a person's behavior may seem to you, for the person engaging in that behavior, it makes sense in their model of the world and is predicated upon satisfying a positive intention for them, though not necessarily for you.

The key is to appreciate that there is a positive intention behind the other person's behavior. This does not mean that you must view the other person's behavior as positive or acceptable. On the contrary, you may find it quite distasteful. You need to look behind the behavior to discover the positive intention or, if it's not apparent, look for an intention that makes sense in their reality. This intention may be for themselves, for you or for someone else. Once you have an understanding of their intention, you can explore alternative ways to help the person achieve it and thus render the unwanted behavior unnecessary.

As an example, let's say your child begins throwing his toys around, while yelling and screaming. I doubt if you would view this as positive behavior. What could possibly be the positive intention behind this kind of behavior? Now look at it from your child's perspective – his model of the world. Perhaps he feels ignored or frustrated because he doesn't know how to figure things out or unsafe because of where he is. Given the resources available to him at that moment, his choice of behavior may have been the only or best option he felt he had – most behaviors are determined at an unconscious level in the blink of an eye. The reasons why he behaved as he did are only guesses. These guesses do give you a starting point as to what may be triggering his behavior and what possible alternative actions you can take – perhaps make him feel he is not being ignored, ensure he has help figuring things out or help him feel safe.

That is, you can accept what happened as feedback, respect his model of the world, explore the possible positive intentions behind his behavior and look at other ways to achieve your outcome while satisfying his positive intention. Be flexible.

Regularly take stock of your own behaviors. Notice the results you are achieving, identify the positive intention behind these behaviors and ask, "Is there a better way to achieve my positive intention?"

A similar way to express this presupposition is: People always do what they believe is right and what works best for their own reality.

9. **Every behavior is appropriate in some context.**
   If your child is throwing a football in your dining room, I am sure you would agree this is not the place to do it and there are other more suitable contexts. You can easily get caught up in either labeling her behavior as bad or even telling your child that *she* is bad. Neither is correct:

   - Labeling a behavior as bad may discourage a child from ever doing it again – in any context. The child, who learns that it is not wise to speak up for herself because she is not being respectful of adults, may not be able to do so when required or as an adult.
   - Labeling a child as bad relates to her identity – who she is – which can cause major problems later on.

   The behavior is not bad and neither is the child, the behavior is simply in the wrong context. You can easily explain to your child in a respectful and supportive manner where and when this behavior is useful and where and when it isn't.

10. **Resistance in another person is a sign of lack of rapport.**
    If your children do not feel safe, either due to your inability to fully explain what is expected of them and the resulting consequences or because of your tone of voice and body language, they may resist your suggestions. Generally, there are no resistant children, only inflexible communicators.

You can simply read the above presuppositions or you can begin to put them into action and make them a way of life. In doing so, you have the opportunity to change your reality, your results and how your family members interact! Here are two methods you may wish to consider:

- Identify a situation in the past in which you did not get the results you desired. Take each presupposition one at a time and review the situation from each of these perspectives. As you do, notice what you can learn about yourself, about others and what other choices are available to you to obtain a different outcome – should a similar circumstance arise in the future.
- Select a different presupposition each time you have a family meeting. Have a discussion among family members about what it means and how it could make a difference within the family.

2.6 TAKING CHARGE OF YOUR LIFE

Do you feel you are a servant to your children or other family members, or do you set clear boundaries and take responsibility for your actions? This is an important distinction and is referred to as being *at effect* or *at cause*. It is the rare individual who always lives her life *at cause*; however, far too many of us live a large portion of our lives *at effect* – responding to the whims, desires or emotional states of others.

Being at cause means you are decisive in creating what you want in life and take responsibility for whatever you achieve. You see the world as a place of opportunity and you move toward achieving what you desire. If things are not unfolding as you would like, you take action and explore other possibilities. Above all, you know you have choice in what you do and how you react to people and events.

If you are at effect, you may blame others or circumstances for your bad moods, for what you have not achieved or for the disarray in your family. You avoid taking responsibility for your actions. You may feel powerless or depend on others in order to feel good about yourself or about life. You may think, "If only my partner, parents, children, friends understood me and helped me achieve my dreams or did what I wanted or what is best for me, then life would be great." If you wait and hope for things to be different or for others to provide you with results or happiness, you are effect, or a victim of circumstances. And really, how satisfying is that? How satisfying do you think it is for others to be around you? Believing that someone else is responsible for your happiness or your different moods is very limiting and gives this person mystical powers over you, which can cause you and often the other person a great deal of anguish.

Being at cause means you have choices in your life. You can choose what is best for you while ensuring the choice is ecological for those around you. That is, you consider the consequences of your actions on others, while not taking responsibility for their emotional well-being. Believing you are responsible for the emotional well-being of someone else places a heavy burden upon you and can cause a great deal of stress.

Those who live their lives at effect often see themselves as victims with no choices whatsoever. The truth is that they do have choices, yet they've chosen not to take action. They are simply reactive to whatever is thrust upon them.

Emotions such as guilt, fear, anxiety and resentment are the result of being at effect. These emotions can wear heavily on your body and your life, and can be the root cause of many physical and personal issues.

Taking responsibility and being at cause for what you create provides an opportunity for significant change, in your relationships with your children, your partner and others.

Do I always live my life at cause? No, not a chance. However, the great majority of the time I do live at cause. When I don't, I use the NLP techniques presented in this book to help me to get back on track, to explore other ways to achieve my outcomes or to ask others for help – without being a victim to their answers.

Each morning when you get up, you can either ask yourself, "I wonder what my day will bring," or "What do I choose to bring to my day?" The life you live and what you create for your children is a function of what you choose.

An exercise

As you do this and other exercises, fully engage it and explore the question, "What will I learn about myself or others?" You may feel a little anxious not knowing what you may discover – stepping into "what you don't know you don't know." This is a journey of self-discovery and all answers are valid. Take your time and fully understand and appreciate the answers you get.

Begin by picking a place in the room that for you represents "100% responsibility" for the issue that you want to gain more clarity on. Step into that space and complete the following sentences out loud. You may do this alone or with a coach:[3]

Face a direction that for you represents the past.

"Looking at the past, this issue reminds me of _____."

Once you have fully considered and completed the above sentence, turn and face a direction that represents the present.

"I keep this an issue in my life by _____."

When you have fully considered this new answer, face a direction that represents the future.

"I can create what I truly desire by _____."

Taking into account what you have learned from completing these three sentences, what actions will you undertake to make a difference in your life and in your relationships with family members?

2.7 THE SECRET ABOUT *THE SECRET*

The Secret (Rhonda Byrne, Atria Books/Beyond Words, 2006) discusses the Law of Attraction, which is to focus on what you want in life.

> You've got to pay attention to what you're attracted
> to, because as you hold images of what you want,
> you're going to be attracted to things and they're

---

3. A coach can be a friend or other family member. Performing this and other exercises with a partner often encourages you to become more involved in the exercise and to be more truthful in your answers.

going to be attracted to you. But it literally moves
into physical reality with and through you.

— Bob Proctor, The Secret

The more precisely you focus, the better the Law of Attraction works. The opposite is also true – the less you focus on what you want, the less you achieve. And what is overlooked and is significant: the more you focus on what you don't want, the more you get of that.

The Law of Attraction does work and it is not a new discovery. Successful men and women have known, used and been writing about this for some time. James Allen, in his book, *As a Man Thinketh* (1902), said,

> Good thoughts and actions can never produce bad results. Bad thoughts and actions can never produce good results. This is but saying that nothing can come from corn but corn, nothing from nettles but nettles. Men understand this law in the natural world, and work with it. But few understand it in the mental and moral world (though its operation there is just as simple and undeviating), and they, therefore, do not cooperate with it.

Using The Law of Attraction to your advantage

Focus your attention and energy on what you want.

If in the past, you tended to focus on the two thousand bits of information that did not support your desires and who you can be, you may wish to play the "opposite game." That is, every time you notice (i.e., interpret) something negative about yourself or other people, reassess your interpretation and look for two things you can interpret as positive and supporting your new view of yourself and the world.

Make this a way of life and encourage your children to do so as well, and you'll find that your world will begin to change, although it may happen slowly at first. Your positive beliefs about yourself, your family and others will strengthen, leading to greater successes.

2.8 YOUR FAMILY SYSTEM

Your family is a system – a group of interacting, interrelated or interdependent elements forming a complex whole. You, your partner and your children are elements or subsystems of the family system and in turn are composed of other subsystems, such as the digestive, immune, respiratory, circulatory, reproductive and nervous systems. As well, your family and each member of your family are members of many different larger systems – extended family, work, school and community. Each system is influenced both by the larger system and its subsystems. For example, if your family environment is chaotic, this may lead to stress. Stress will affect your immune system, which will have an impact on your health. On the other hand, a chaotic family environment will bleed into the larger systems and affect how you and your family function within these systems. That is, your actions or lack of action affect much more than just you.

The components of a family system – you, your partner and your children – continually adjust their interactions to maintain what is perceived to be stability for the system – in other words, that which is familiar – to avoid the unknown. If in reading this book or taking a workshop on personal growth, your actions are perceived as changing the family dynamic, your partner or children may choose to discount what you have learned or bring up other ideas that will maintain or bring your family system back to "stability," or what is already known. In an alcoholic or dysfunctional family, other family members may take on co-dependent behaviors to create the illusion of "normal" or stable, which in turn influences the creation of yet other systems – a high percentage of children from alcoholic families become addicts themselves or marry alcoholics.

Each of us is a living system. If one part of the system is changed, other parts must adapt. Given this fact, consider the following. What if you misinterpreted a significant past event – an event that led you to make limiting decisions about yourself, your parenting skills and about others? Given the resources you have as an adult and what you know today, what would happen if you reassessed that event and came to a different understanding or decision? Would this not change how you parent, how you perceive and respond to life now and in the future? This idea of conscious awareness, change and subsequent growth is addressed throughout this book.

Ecology

Ecology is the relationship between subsystems and with the larger system. In NLP, before making a change or committing to an outcome, it's important to check the ecology of the proposed change. That is, you need to be consciously aware of the effects and consequences of your proposed actions on yourself, your health, your family and your community. This does not mean you should give in to others' demands or needs. It simply means that before committing to a new course of action, you are aware of the consequences of not proceeding, as well as the consequences of your proposed actions. You may then wish to explore whether there is another way in which you can achieve the same desired result while minimizing the perceived negative consequences on your health or for other people in your life.

If your child is exhibiting a behavior that you do not appreciate, take a look at what's happening from a system perspective. Instead of focusing on one child and what he is doing to the exclusion of everything else, looking at the family dynamic as a whole often provides insights about the reasons behind the unwanted behavior and possible remedial actions and their consequences.

2.9 OTHER THINGS TO CONSIDER

This section provides the remaining pieces that will support your basic understanding and enjoyment of the material in this book.

Content free

Many of the NLP techniques are content free. That is, your children or partner do not have to tell you their "story." Although some understanding of the issue will help, you do not need all the details. Some people prefer not to reveal too many details, while others revel in telling the story. However, they may have told the story so many times that it has become a rote exercise, and occasionally they may embellish in order to give it a little more zing. Having told their story so often, some people may begin to accept this embellished story as reality.

Break state

For many of the NLP techniques, a critical step is used called *break state*. Quite simply, you want the child or partner you're coaching to clear her mind of the internal representations she was making and go to a neutral state. This is easily done by making a statement or asking a question such as the following: "Do you like my shirt?" What you're wearing does not matter. She will look to see what you're wearing, which will clear her mind of the previous internal representations. Other questions or statements might be: "Do you like the color of this wall?" or "Oh, look the sun is shining." As well, you can ask your partner or child to stand or to stretch (remember, physiology affects internal representations).

Future pacing

Future pacing is often the last step in an NLP technique and is used to verify that the changes have taken effect. Your child or partner has gone through the NLP technique and made the changes that he desires. Now you ask him to go out into the future, where a similar situation to the problem scenario may arise, and to describe how he feels or reacts given his new choices, knowledge and resources. Use your sensory acuity to notice any shifts that may indicate that he is not fully congruent with these new choices or behavior. If he is not fully congruent, additional work will be necessary.

Future pacing is also a mental rehearsal that provides an opportunity to see the future from a more positive perspective. Mentally rehearsing the successful completion of a future situation significantly increases the possibility of success.

You may want to do this several times – further convincing him that the change has been made.

Why NLP techniques may not work

There are a number of reasons why NLP techniques may not work. The three most important reasons are:

- Lack of safety. You have not established rapport or a feeling of trust with your children or partner, have not adequately explained the technique and approach they will be using, or the environment is perceived as unsafe. If they do not feel safe, while they may go through the motions, they will not step into the unknown and make the changes they desire.

- Secondary gain. Your children will manifest certain undesirable (to you) behaviors because, in their model of the world, they see some benefit. From the perspective of an outsider, this so-called benefit may seem harmful, silly or irrelevant. What is important is how they perceive their reality, not another person's perception of what it may be. If this secondary gain is not addressed or satisfied in some other manner, they will eventually revert to their old behaviors to get this benefit.

  For example, your child may dress in "interesting" ways. He says he is comfortable in these clothes and perhaps that's true. What if he dresses this way to get attention or to feel like he is part of a group? If this is true, until this unspoken secondary gain is addressed, you have little chance of getting him to dress differently.

- Desired change is not in alignment with the higher *logical levels* (see section 3.5: The hidden traits that influence how you interact with others). Let's suppose your child wishes to change his behavior when speaking in front of his classmates. At present he has a deeply rooted belief that he is not good enough. If he fails to address the higher-level belief issues, any behavioral change he makes will eventually be overridden by these deep-rooted beliefs.

A word of caution

NLP techniques are very powerful. However, the true power comes from the proficiency of the person using them. Just as a world-class racecar driver can do things with her car that you and I can only dream about and should not attempt, so it is with the NLP techniques. I recommend that you practice these techniques in a safe environment, such as under the guidance of a fully qualified professional. Taking an NLP seminar is a good way to begin.

Cars bring a measure of value (and some detrimental effects) to each of us and our society. A car in the hands of someone who does not follow the rules of the road nor considers the safety and well-being of others is a serious problem and a threat to others. It's easy to see that it's not the car that's at fault, it's the person who is using the car inappropriately. So too with NLP. Please use the NLP techniques with integrity and, if in doubt, seek the advice of qualified professionals.

2.10 OVERVIEW OF THIS CHAPTER

Mind maps – developed by Tony Buzan (*The Mind Map Book*, Plume, 1996) – are included at the end of each chapter to provide a quick review and to assist you in recalling the material presented.

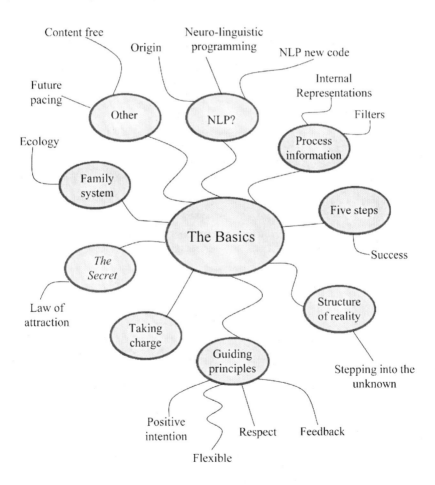

FIGURE 3: MIND MAP OF THIS CHAPTER:
UNDERSTANDING THE BASICS

3.

Getting to Know Yourself and Others

3.1 ACCESSING AND PROCESSING INFORMATION

Representational systems

At any given moment, your five sensory modalities (the *neuro* of neuro-linguistic programming) have access to about four billion bits of information. These modalities are visual (V), auditory (A), kinesthetic (K), gustatory (G) and olfactory (O). Kinesthetic can be external – tactile sensations like touch, temperature and moisture, or internal – emotions and inner feelings of balance and body awareness. The modalities are also used to record (remember) your perceptions of your "outside world" – the two thousand bits you pay attention to and perceive to be important, of interest or relevant. These recordings in your mind (pictures, sounds, feelings, tastes and smells) are called *internal representations*. Thus, the modalities are often referred to as *representational systems* (or rep systems) – the primary way you represent, code, store and give meaning or language (the *linguistic* of NLP) to your experiences.

Of the five representational systems, visual, auditory and kinesthetic are used and discussed most often in NLP. Although primary senses, gustatory and olfactory do not play a major role and are often included with kinesthetic. However, if you are addressing an issue that involves taste or smell (e.g., food) or you are a person who uses and relies on your gustatory or olfactory senses to a large degree, these senses need to be considered separate from kinesthetic. Many NLP practitioners split the auditory system into two components: auditory tonal (A_t – sound) and auditory digital (A_d – words as separate verbal symbols or digits).

You can access more than one representational system at the same time; for example, you can listen to music (A_t) while seeing a picture of a friend in your mind's eye (V). As you will discover when we cover strategies that your behavior is produced from a mixture of internal and external sensory experiences.

Preferred representational systems

You use all of your senses and, at any given time, depending upon the circumstances, you may focus on one or more of them. When listening to a favorite piece of music, for instance, you may close your eyes to more fully listen and to experience certain deeper feelings.

Each of us has one or more preferred representational systems. When learning something new, you may prefer to see it or imagine it performed, while some people need to hear how to do it, others need to get a feeling for it and yet others have to make sense of it. In general, one system is not better than another. However, depending on the context, one or more of the representational systems may be more effective. Landscape painters will tend to use visual modalities; musicians, auditory tonal; athletes, kinesthetic; and mathematicians, auditory digital. People at the top of their profession typically have the ability to use all of the representational systems and to choose the one most appropriate for the situation.

Depending on your preferred representational system(s), you may exhibit certain behaviors or characteristics. Before exploring these behaviors, note that, depending on what is going on in your life – the context – you may change your preferred representational system(s) from time to time. Hence, it is useful to notice the representational system your partner or children are currently favoring and refer to it as a current preference rather than limiting their potential by permanently labeling them as visual, auditory, etc.

The following are generalizations of the characteristics of people with a preference for visual, auditory tonal, kinesthetic or auditory digital representational systems. Remember, as with all generalizations, there are always exceptions.

Visual
People with a visual preference will tend to:

- Be organized, neat and well-groomed. Why? Because they want to *look* good. And what do they expect from you? Yes, the same thing.
- Use *visualization* for memory and decision-making – often getting *insights* about something.
- Be more *imaginative* and may have difficulty putting their ideas in words.
- Speak faster than the general population. Why? Because they have a *picture(s)* in their mind and, if it is a moving *picture*, there is much to tell in a relatively short time.

- Talk about seemingly disjointed topics, yet in their mind they can *see* the *picture* that *shows* they are all connected.
- Prefer in-person interactions – to *see* the other person and her reactions.
- Want to *see* or be *shown* concepts, ideas or how something is done.
- Want to *see* the big *picture*.
- Not remember what others have said, and become confused if they are given too many verbal instructions. However, if you draw a *map* or *picture* for them, they can *see* what you're saying.
- Remember faces more easily than names.
- Be distracted by *visual* activity and less so by noise.

Auditory tonal (for simplicity, referred to as auditory)
People with an auditory preference will tend to:

- Be more aware of subtle change in the *tone* of your *voice* and be more responsive to certain *tones* of *voice*.
- Perceive and represent sequences and are able to remember directions or instructions more easily.
- Learn by *listening* and *asking* questions.
- Enjoy *discussions* and prefer to communicate through *spoken* language rather than the written word.
- *Talk* through problems and like to have someone available to serve as a *sounding* board for their ideas.
- Need to be *heard*.
- Be easily distracted by *noise*.

Kinesthetic
People with a kinesthetic preference will tend to:

- Speak slower than the average person. Why? Because they need time to get in *touch* with how they *feel* about the topic.
- Be more sensitive to their *bodies* and their *feelings* and respond to *physical* rewards and *touching*.
- Learn by *doing, moving* or *touching*.
- Dress and groom themselves for *comfort* rather than for appearance.
- Make decisions based on their *feelings*.
- Stand closer to other people than those with a visual preference in order to *feel* the other person's *energy*, whereas the person with a visual preference will stand back to observe more of the other person's body language.

Auditory digital
The auditory digital modality is devoid of the physical senses. People with an auditory digital preference will tend to:

- Have a need to make *sense* of the world, to *figure* things out, to *understand* concepts.
- Talk to themselves and carry on conversations with you in their mind. They may say they recall discussing something with you, when the conversation actually never took place. However, to the auditory digital person, a mental conversation with you is very real.
- Learn by working things out in their minds.
- Not be spontaneous, as they like to *think* things through.
- Have *logic, facts* and *figures* play a key role in the *decision*-making process.
- Memorize by *steps, procedures* and *sequences*.

I have a PhD in statistics. Does this give you some idea as to my preferred representational system, at least when I was working on my PhD? Remember, I may have changed my preferences over time. If you said auditory digital (facts and figures, logic), you are partially correct. I also had a preference for visual, although this modality was weaker than auditory digital; I was able to visualize mathematical formulations in my mind and work them through before committing them to paper. Many scientists and inventors have a highly developed ability to visualize.

Can you see yourself in one or more of these representational systems? Does one sound better than the others, do you feel one is a better fit than another or is one more logical? A small preference test is available at www.renewal.ca/nlp11.htm to give you an indication of your preferred representational system(s).

How does a preference for one or more of the representational systems become established or change over time? Quite simply, it is based on the principle that we tend to move toward what we perceive as pleasure or reward and away from what we perceive as punishment or pain. As a child, if you were praised for your artistry or ability to combine visually appealing colors, you would tend to do more of this or similar activities. On the other hand, if your music abilities went unnoticed or were criticized, you may have tended to discount this modality and move to one of the others. An auditory digital preference may result from earning high praise for your ability to figure things out and work with facts and figures.

Since you are continually moving toward pleasure and away from pain, your preferences change over time or can be different in different contexts – it all depends on how you interpret an event and what you perceive to be pleasure and pain.

Instead of labeling yourself as strictly visual, auditory, kinesthetic or auditory digital, consider putting effort into developing the other representational systems. Giving you the potential to experience the world in new and different ways, which may lead to greater opportunities.

How can you encourage your children to develop a proficiency in each of the representational systems? You can provide them with toys and activities that stimulate them from a visual, auditory, kinesthetic, auditory digital, olfactory and gustatory perspective, while providing supportive, positive, reinforcing feedback. Currently, you may be drawn to or find it easier to provide toys and activities for your children that are based on your preferred representational system(s). To further develop an existing representational system that seems to be weak, it comes down to the old saying "practice makes perfect." If you score low on visual, start paying attention to what is in your visual field – the different colors and shapes and how they blend together or not.

Identifying a person's preferences

To identify a person's preferences, pay attention to the behaviors listed above for visual, auditory, kinesthetic and auditory digital representational systems. Listen for the words they use and watch their eye patterns.

What do you notice about the following four sentences?

- This toy looks very good. I'd like to see how it works.
- This toy sounds very good. I'd like to hear how it works.
- This toy feels very good. I'd like to get a handle on how it works.
- This toy makes good sense. I'd like more details on how it works.

The first sentence uses visual words, the second auditory, the third kinesthetic and the fourth uses words that are not sensory based (auditory digital), yet all four sentences convey the same general meaning.

You use words to describe your thoughts. If your thoughts – your internal representations – are mainly pictures, you will tend to use more visual words when describing your thoughts. If the basis of your thoughts is logic or making sense of something, you will tend to use words that reflect the logic of your thinking. Likewise for auditory and kinesthetic. The words you use reflect your internal thought processes. That is, you convey the form of your internal thoughts and thought structures to others through the words you choose to use.

In NLP terms, visual, auditory, kinesthetic and auditory digital words and phrases are called *predicates*. The words a person uses provide you with an indication of that person's preferred representational system. The following are examples of visual, auditory, kinesthetic and auditory digital words. This is not a complete list. Can you think of other words or phrases that might be added? Notice that some words like *fuzzy* can appear in more than one column.

Visual	Auditory	Kinesthetic	Auditory Digital
see	hear	grasp	sense
look	tell	feel	experience
bright	sound	hard	understand
clear	resonate	unfeeling	change
picture	listen	concrete	perceive
foggy	silence	scrape	question
view	deaf	solid	sensitive
focused	squeak	fuzzy	distinct
fuzzy	hush	get hold of	conceive
dawn	roar	catch on	know
reveal	melody	tap into	think
illuminate	make music	heated argument	learn
imagine	harmonize	pull some strings	process
hazy	tune in/out	sharp as a tack	decide
an eyeful	rings a bell	smooth operator	motivate
short-sighted	quite as a mouse	make contact	consider
take a peek	voice an opinion	firm foundation	describe in detail
tunnel vision	clear as a bell	get a handle on	figure it out
bird's eye view	give me your ear	get in touch with	make sense of
naked eye	loud and clear	hand in hand	word for word
paint a picture	purr like a kitten	hang in there	without a doubt

No matter what your preferred representational system, you use visual, auditory, kinesthetic and auditory digital words all the time. Some contexts imply the use of one type; for example, if I asked you to describe a painting, you would likely use more visual words. And, if there is a choice, you will tend to use words from your preferred representational system.

Sometimes we don't speak the same language

Have you ever explained something to someone, who responded with, "I don't see what you are saying" or "I can't picture this." What is at work here? One possibility is that the person is highly visual. You, however, have been using words other than visual; hence, your listener is having difficulty forming a picture of your explanation in her mind. And how do we usually handle this situation? We repeat the same words, only this time with emphasis, as if our listener had heard nothing the first time around!

Given what you've learned thus far about NLP, how might you approach this situation differently so your listener can *see* what you are saying? One possibility is to use visual words to help her form a picture in her mind, or you may wish to draw a diagram or picture.

Of course, it's not just visual people who may have difficulty with your explanation. An auditory person may say, "This doesn't sound right." A kinesthetic person may say, "I don't have a feeling for this." An auditory digital person, "This doesn't make sense."

If you pay attention to the words people are using, you'll find they reveal to you how they see, hear, get in touch with or make sense of the world around them.

Interacting with others

Think about a time when you first started dating your partner. You probably made certain you looked good by dressing and grooming appropriately; you and your date went to places to see attractions; you used appropriate voice tonalities and enjoyed the music; you touched and held hands; you made sure that you smelled good and visited different restaurants to taste different foods. In other words, you used all the representational systems to suitably impress and charm your date.

At some point, you moved beyond the "dating" stage and became partners or perhaps got married. And often, instead of using all the representational systems or sensory modalities, you and your partner reverted to the representational systems that you each prefer and that may not be the same. If you are visual, you may want to get dressed up to go out and see a show, and expect and give gifts that are visually appealing – including the wrapping. If your partner, on the other hand, is kinesthetic, they want to dress comfortably, touch and hold hands, and give and receive gifts that exude a feeling. If you and your partner do not learn to express your individual needs and expectations in terms of your preferred representational systems, as well as showing flexibility in satisfying each other's needs in their preferred representational system, you each may be in for a difficult ride. Has this happened to you?

Now, what about your children? Are you interacting with them in terms of their preferred representational systems or yours?

Listen to the words that family members use. They will use a mixture of visual, auditory, kinesthetic and auditory digital words, and one or two of these will be used more frequently. This gives an indication of their preferred representational system. Be aware that if you ask them a visual-based question – for example, to describe a painting – no matter what their preference, they will use many visual words. To determine their preferred representational systems, be sure the questions you ask are not biased to one particular modality.

Rapport with others is very important. One way to increase your rapport is to match the words they use. That is, if they use mainly kinesthetic words in their speech, you ideally use more kinesthetic words when speaking to them.

Improving your ability to access all representational systems

To improve your ability and that of your children to use all representational systems, you may want to undertake the following: For two minutes, describe your home or pet using only visual words. Repeat using only auditory words, followed by kinesthetic words and finally auditory digital words. Hint: for visual, you can describe different colors; for auditory, different sounds; for kinesthetic, different feelings or textures; and for auditory digital, use facts and figures. Notice which modality (or modalities) gives the most difficulty. These are the ones that will need practice. For people to clearly see, hear, grasp and understand your message, you need to be able to speak their language.

You can assist your children in accessing a less frequently used representational system by using a process called *overlap*. Your child may say that he cannot visualize, yet has no problem accessing feelings or sounds in his mind. If he enjoys going to the beach, have him remember what it feels like to walk across a cool, wet sandy beach in his bare feet, feeling the warm sun on his body and the gentle breeze on his face. As he gets into these feelings, begin to introduce sounds, such as the sound of the waves on the beach and seagulls in the distance. Now begin to intersperse visual sights in between the kinesthetic and auditory cues and have him notice that he does indeed have visual memories of this experience. Continue to repeat this type of exercise until he can easily visualize different events.

3.2 EYE ACCESSING CUES

Have you ever noticed that people's eyes move when they are thinking? This is valuable information that can provide you with clues as to whether they are thinking in pictures, sounds, feelings or talking to themselves. It is information about their preferred representational systems.

According to neurological research (Ehrlichman, H., & Weinberger, A. [1978] "Lateral eye movements and hemispheric asymmetry: A critical review." *Psychological Bulletin*, 86, 1080–1101), eye movement both laterally and vertically seems to be associated with activating different parts of the brain. In the neurological literature, these movements are called lateral eye movements (LEM), and in NLP, we call them *eye accessing cues* because they give us insights into how people are accessing information.

Auditory digital
- What is something you continually tell yourself?
- What are your thoughts about this book?

Kinesthetic
- What does it feel like to walk barefoot on a cool, wet sandy beach?
- What does it feel like when you rub your fingers on sandpaper?

People's eyes do not always move
Sometimes people's eyes do not move. This may be due to:

- The "look-to-talk" rule. That is, when you are making eye contact with some people, they will return your gaze directly, and their eyes will seem not to move, or move only very slightly and quickly. In this situation, they may be defocusing their eyes so their "internal" eye can look in the appropriate direction.
- Near-term memory. If the answer is something that is well-known to the person – their own name, for example – or is a recent observation, they will not need to search their minds for the answer and their eyes will not move.

Using eye patterns to assess congruence

If a person is describing something they have seen or heard, their eyes should primarily move to visual or auditory remembered. However, if a person is inventing something, their eyes will tend to move to visual or auditory constructed, indicating they are constructing some part of the situation being described. This may indicate that the person is uncertain or untruthful about what they are thinking, or they may be projecting something in the future.

Be careful in assuming someone is untruthful. For example, suppose you ask me a question about something I had never thought about before. To formulate an answer, I may have to look at or hear one or more pieces of true information in a way I have never done before. In this situation, I would be constructing an answer and my eyes would most likely move to visual or auditory constructed.

Preferred representational systems

People's eye movements relate to their preferred representational systems. If you have a high preference for visual, your eyes will often go up to see images in your mind. Or, if you have a high preference for kinesthetic, your eyes will often move down to get in touch with your feelings.

And it is not quite as simple as I just alluded to. If your conversation is focused on something visual, no matter what your preference, your eyes will move up from time to time. Also, there is a *lead representational system*, which may not be the same as your preferred representational system. Simply put, your lead system is the way you first access information and bring it to your conscious mind. For example, if your lead system is visual, and I asked you what it feels like to be in a nice, warm bath, you would likely form a picture of being in the bath before accessing the feeling itself.

Remember, your preferred representational system is the sensory modality – visual, auditory, kinesthetic or auditory digital – you use to organize and understand some experience or situation. If I am speaking to someone and I notice that their eyes keep going up to visual, even if I am not using visual words or pictures, this is a clue that they may be forming visual internal representations; therefore, their preferred representational system is most likely visual. To assist them in creating this picture in their mind, I could use more visual words when speaking. On the other hand, if their eyes are tracking on the horizontal plane, this means they are processing in sounds, and their preferred representational system maybe auditory. If their eyes move downward, they may be processing kinesthetically or attempting to make logical sense of what I am saying (auditory digital). If, in addition, their eyes move downward to the right and they are right-handed, their preferred representational system is most likely kinesthetic.

A thought for teachers (and parents)

Some teachers expect a student to look at them when asked a question. If, in response to a question from the teacher, your child looks up to "see" the answer, the teacher may respond with, "The answer is not on the ceiling, so look at me." In this situation, your child may not be able to answer the teacher, because she is not allowed to look up to "see" the answer.

Building your confidence in reading eye accessing cues

There are a number of ways to practice reading eye accessing cues. Here are two:

- With their permission, practice with your friends and family members. Watch their eye accessing cues and then verify your observations with them.
- Watch talk shows on TV (be sure the show is spontaneous and not rehearsed). This is a great way to practice – you can stare at the people on the TV and it will not bother them at all. Notice whether there is a relationship between where the person looks and the words they use. For instance, if the person's eyes are looking up, do they tend to use more visual words?

3.3 PAYING ATTENTION

Are you consciously aware of what is going on around you or inside of you? Are you just going through the motions of living? Are you paying attention to the subtle clues that can turn a meaningless conversation into something worthwhile? Are you responding to the opportunities that are there – if you were to take a moment to see, hear, feel or experience them? Are you listening to your internal signals when it comes to taking action, or are you doing what you think others expect or demand of you? Perhaps it's time to begin paying attention to these signals.

Here's an example. Recently, by using my sensory acuity, I was available to avoid a potentially nasty situation. My wife questioned me on something about which she has a good deal of knowledge. As I was answering her question, I realized from her body language and facial expressions that she didn't understand what I was saying. Being flexible, I changed my approach, yet she still wasn't getting it. Fortunately, I was also paying attention to what was going on inside of me. I could feel my frustration building and before I let it express itself in an unfortunate choice of words, tone of voice or body language, I said to her, "Would you like to go to the basement and I can show you what I mean?" Immediately her facial expression changed to a warm and welcoming smile of acceptance. By paying attention to how my wife was reacting and to my internal signals, I was able to avoid a potentially unpleasant situation.

Sensory acuity – seeing, hearing, feeling (physically and emotionally), smelling and tasting – is a critical piece of NLP and your life. Whether you're a parent or child, when interacting with others or enjoying a moment with yourself, it's important for you to be aware of:

- Feedback/information that indicates the extent to which you are on or off target in achieving your outcomes.
- Other people's actions and reactions to certain situations/stimuli.
- How you are reacting to certain situations/stimuli.

The third step of the five steps for success is to pay attention and have some form of measure to know whether you're making progress toward your desired outcomes. What are the signs (visual, auditory, kinesthetic, olfactory or gustatory) that indicate whether you are on course? If you are not, what corrective action is required? If you don't use your sensory acuity, you may end up far off course or spend more effort than is required. For example, have you ever discovered after an interaction that you did not pay attention to what was important to a loved one? Or perhaps you failed to heed warning signs and missed a potential opportunity to establish a meaningful relationship or provide much needed support.

Often we pay attention through our preferred representational system and miss subtle or even obvious changes available through the other representational systems that may be critical for achieving our outcomes or avoiding problems.

Observing other people's actions and reactions

Whether you're having a conversation with your child, providing support to a friend, delivering a presentation to your local parent-teacher association, negotiating with another person or sharing an intimate moment with a loved one, it's important to understand how people experience the world around them. You need to recognize their preferred representational systems to more clearly express your ideas so they can see, hear or get in touch with your message. You should also be perceptive about changes in another person's physiology, tone of voice and energy that may indicate a change in their internal thoughts or emotional state. In these situations, you may need to stop what you're doing and alter your approach. Yet how often do you miss these signals and continue doing what you've always done, somehow expecting different results the next time?

When observing other people, you will want to notice:

- Words they use (predicates).
- Eye movements (eye accessing cues).
- Changes in skin color and tone.
- Breathing.
- Voice quality and tone.
- Posture and gestures.
- Changes in energy – many people with kinesthetic as a preferred representational system or who are visually impaired are "highly" attuned to changes in energy. We all have the ability to do this; we simply have not taken the time to practice the skill.

Paying attention to your internal and external signals

Often we do not pay attention to what is going on inside ourselves. How often have you had an instinctive (body) reaction that said, "No, don't do this!" or "Yes, this is what I really want to do!" but you ignored it and later regretted your action or inaction. For some of us, the internal signals or physiological reactions are present, but we are just not aware of them – perhaps because we have ignored them for such a long time that they are now out of our conscious awareness.

Some of the internal or physiological responses to which you could start paying attention are:

- Holding your breath. Do you hold your breath when you are stressed? When you hold your breath, your body does not get enough oxygen, which causes even more stress. When you notice you are holding your breath, take this as a signal to give yourself permission to breathe deeply at a relaxed pace.
- A tightening in your stomach or chest.
- A certain pain or twitch.

- A feeling of joy, love or accomplishment – or are these the feelings you tend to ignore?
- Internal representations (images and sounds) you create in your mind.

Be aware of what is going on inside of you. Your interaction with others is a reflection of your internal thoughts and beliefs. If you do not feel resourceful or good about yourself, this will be evident in your conversation with those you love through your choice of words, your tone of voice, your body language and the energy emanating from you. Even if your children are not consciously aware of these signals coming from you, they will sense them at an unconscious level and react to them in some way.

> Tell me to what you pay attention
> and I will tell you who you are.
>
> – *Jose Ortega y Gasset*

Practicing your sensory acuity

This is a two-person exercise that you can have fun doing with your family. Let's call the two people Ryan and Sarah. Sarah's job is simply to observe Ryan.

1. Ryan closes his eyes and thinks of someone he dislikes.

2. While Ryan thinks about this person, he begins at the top of his head and slowly moves his attention down his own body, noticing any physiological reaction to thinking about this person. For instance, he may notice tension around his eyes, a pain in his shoulder or a heavy feeling in his stomach. As he scans his body, he tells Sarah what he is observing.

3. Once Ryan has finished describing what he has observed, Sarah tells Ryan what she has observed. For example, she may have observed his eyes closed tightly, a red flushing around his neck, very shallow breathing, twitching of a finger on his right hand, a certain tone of voice or an energy pushing her away from him.

4. Once step three is completed, Ryan stretches and/or looks around the room – a break state – and clears his mind of the internal representations of the person he dislikes.

5. Ryan closes his eyes and repeats steps two and three while thinking of someone he likes.

6. Again, he creates a break state by stretching or looking around the room.

7. Ryan may find he is surprised at the different internal and external reactions he had between thinking of someone he dislikes and someone he likes. He may also be surprised by the reactions he was not aware of – those that

Sarah described to him. As a result of this exercise, Ryan may discover that he really does telegraph his feelings and thoughts to others, even if it is at an unconscious level.

8. Ryan chooses one of the two people he had been thinking about earlier, and this time, he does not tell Sarah which person it is. He closes his eyes again and thinks of this person.

9. From what she had observed earlier, Sarah tells Ryan who he is thinking about. Almost like magic!

A caution

For sensory acuity, you must stick with what you have seen, heard, felt, tasted or smelled. You should not project an opinion or guess. For example, you may observe that your child's lips curl up at the ends in the form of smile, which is a fact. You may then tell her that she is happy, which is a guess, a hallucination or a mind read. The smile may be a result of the fact that she has any number of things taking place mentally or physiologically.

Mind-reading has the potential to get you into trouble. Consider the difference between your child when he is angry versus when he is very determined and focused on completing a task. The external physiological cues may be quite similar. If you ask your focused and determined child why he is angry, he may indeed get angry with you for making an erroneous judgment about him.

3.4 UNCONSCIOUS MOTIVATORS

Recall that at any given moment you have access to four billion bits of information, yet you only focus consciously on the two thousand that you perceive to be important – that is, the information that is in alignment with your beliefs/ values or preferred representational system. *Meta programs* are another important set of filters that determine how you perceive the world around you. Meta programs are deeply rooted, unconscious mental programs that automatically filter your experiences and guide and direct your thought processes, resulting in significant differences in how you communicate with others and the behaviors you manifest.

Early researchers noticed that two people with similar meta programs were able to quickly develop rapport with each other. On the other hand, if the meta programs were not aligned, people found it difficult to understand or agree with each other.

Originally about sixty different patterns were identified. Fortunately, subsequent researchers have combined many of these to form a much smaller and more useful set. The number and descriptions of the patterns vary slightly from author to author. I prefer to use the fourteen meta programs as described by Rodger Bailey. He determined that people who have the same language profile (choice of words, body language) generally have the same behavior patterns and vice versa. Hence, on the basis of the words a person uses, you can make predictions about her behavior. Also, once you have determined the person's behavior patterns, you can choose specific words that will have the most influence on her. Bailey called his set of meta programs the Language and Behavior Profile (LAB Profile). In this book, I have chosen to discuss the five meta programs that Bailey calls *motivation traits*. For a more extensive discussion on the LAB Profile, particularly in a business context, see Shelle Rose Charvet's *Words that Change Minds: Mastering the Language of Influence*, Kendal Hunt, 1997.

Some points to consider
- Meta programs may vary across contexts – school or home – and may change over time as you learn new information or experience significant events in your life. The meta programs you exhibit today or in a particular context represent a current preference.
- Each meta program represents a continuum from one extreme to another. For some meta programs, you may be positioned in the middle, between the two extremes. For other meta programs, you may be at one of the extremes. If you have difficulty imagining or relating to someone who lives their life as described by one extreme of a meta program, you are probably at the other end of the range. On the other hand, if you relate entirely to one of these descriptions, this is most likely true for you.
- When you communicate, your natural tendency is to explain yourself in ways that correspond to how you best understand or interpret the world (meta programs). Often this will not create any major difficulty. However, if your child's thinking or experience of the world is significantly different from yours, communicating with him via your preferred meta programs can result in a communication disconnect, potentially making it difficult for him to fit into the family or for you to support him. To have a meaningful conversation or relationship with family members who have different meta programs, you need to respect their model of the world, be flexible and speak to them in their language.

As you read the following meta programs, you are encouraged to identify your preferences and those of your family members. Also notice how your choice of meta programs affects how you live your life and the interaction you have with others. Use this information to improve your communication and the support you provide to your partner and children. In each case, I have described the extremes and it may well be that you or your family member is in the middle – exhibiting characteristics from both extremes.

1. Toward – Away From

Are your children motivated by goals and achievements or by issues and problems to be resolved or avoided?

Toward: These people are focused on their goals. They are motivated to have, achieve and attain. Although they tend to be good at managing priorities, they sometimes have trouble recognizing what should be avoided or identifying problems that can get them into trouble. They are clear in what they want. You will hear them use words such as: accomplish, attain, get, achieve, rewards, and they will speak about achieving goals, results and outcomes. To motivate or influence these people, use the words that they use in a context of achieving.

These people do not consciously look for mistakes. If your children have a Toward preference, their homework may have numerous unnecessary errors, simply because they are focused on getting it done so they can achieve or do something else. In this situation, you may wish to point out that addressing their errors is a first step toward achieving what they desire. While children with a Toward preference can benefit from the help of an Away From parent, this is the very type they will tend to avoid, because the Away From parent often tells them what may go wrong or what has to be fixed without allowing them to fully express their ideas.

A Toward parent – working to achieve, attain, get – may not have time to spend with his children or may encourage his children to achieve at the cost of them having time to enjoy being children and playing with their friends.

Away From: People in this group often see only what may go wrong in a given situation – notice what should be eliminated, avoided or repaired. They are motivated when there is a problem to be solved or trouble in need of fixing. They are good at troubleshooting, solving problems and pinpointing possible obstacles because they automatically see what is wrong. They may set goals or priorities; however, they will abandon them immediately if there is a pressing problem. These people will tend to use words such as: avoid, steer clear of, prevent, eliminate, solve, get rid of, fix, prohibit. And these are exactly the words you can use to motivate them to get something done. You can motivate your children who have an Away From preference by noting that doing a specific activity or achieving an outcome will help them to avoid or fix a perceived negative consequence. At times your children may be distracted and operate from a crisis management perspective as there are so many things to be fixed.

If you have a preference for Toward and your children have a tendency for Away From, they may find your behaviors annoying as you may be overwhelming them with things they can achieve, while not allowing them to fix perceived problems. On the other hand, if you have a tendency for Away From and are always noticing what doesn't work, you may turn your children off as they may decide "Why bother? I'm going to get heck if I do this or if I don't."

We all have habits – some serve us and others get in the way or bring undesired consequences. To break an unwanted habit, you need both short-term (Away From) and long-term (Toward) motivation. The Away From gets you moving away from what you don't want and loses its influence once you've begun your journey. That is, in the longer term, without Toward motivation to keep you moving toward something you desire, eventually you will find yourself back where you began or something similar to it.

2. Internal – External

Does your partner assess her work through her own internal standards and beliefs? Do your children judge their performance through information and feedback from external sources?

Internal: These people have internal standards and make their own judgments about the quality of their work. They have difficulty accepting other people's opinions and outside direction. If they receive negative feedback regarding something they believe they have done well, they will question the judgment of the person giving the feedback. As a result, they may be difficult to manage. They assess information from outside sources according to their own internal standards. You can motivate this type of person with the following phrases: you know what's best, only you can decide, it is up to you, I need your opinion. For example, "I was thinking of doing [a certain task], and I would like your opinion." or "Here are some possible approaches. What are your thoughts?" Since they do not need feedback on their own progress, Internals tend not to give feedback to others.

External: People in this group need to receive outside direction and feedback to stay motivated and to know how well they are doing. Without external validation, they may feel lost or have difficulty starting or continuing an activity. They may interpret a simple discussion as an order and then feel overwhelmed with all you have directed them to do. They are motivated by phrases such as: according to the experts, your friends will think highly of you, you will be recognized for your efforts, your teacher will be pleased to see how well you have done your homework. An externally referenced child with an internally referenced parent may be at a loss to know how well she is doing.

To identify whether your children are Internal or External, ask them a question such as, "At school, how do you know you have written a good essay?" An Internal child may say, "I just know or it feels right." An External child may say, "My teacher needs to give me a good mark, say nice things or smile at me." And a child with a balanced Internal – External, may say a combination of the two.

3. Options – Procedures

Do your children prefer to keep their options open and explore alternatives or do they feel most comfortable following established procedures?

Options: People in this group are motivated by the possibility of doing something in an alternative way. They are the type of people who will develop procedures and not follow them. They enjoy breaking or bending the rules. Exploring new ideas and possibilities is of great interest. They may begin a new project and not feel compelled to finish it. To motivate or influence these people, use words and phrases such as: alternatives, break the rules, flexibility, unlimited possibilities, expand your choices, options. Listen for these words to help you identify this type of person. If your child has a preference for Options, make sure she has choice and you are flexible (while still maintaining your standards).

Procedures: These people like to follow established rules and processes. Once they understand a procedure, they will follow it repeatedly. They have great difficulty developing new processes and feel lost without a clearly defined way to do something. They are more concerned about how to do something than about why they should do it. Bending or breaking rules is sacrilege! They are motivated by words and phrases such as: correct way, tried and true, first/then, lastly, proven path. A Procedures child will be more comfortable with routine and clearly defined ways to do things. An environment where the rules or ways of doing things are not clearly defined or changing will be upsetting for a Procedures-oriented child, and she may complain she doesn't know how to do what you have requested.

4. Proactive – Reactive/Reflective

Do your children tend to initiate or prefer to wait for others to lead?

Proactive: People in this group tend to initiate and not wait for others. From a Reactive's point of view, they act with little or no consideration, jump into situations without thinking or analyzing and bulldoze ahead with their own agenda. They excel at getting the job done. To motivate or influence these people, use phrases such as: go for it, just do it, why wait, take charge, what are you waiting for. To identify these people, notice whether they use short sentences with an active verb, speak as if they are in control or have difficulty sitting still for long periods.

Reactive/Reflective: These people have a tendency to wait for others to initiate or until the situation is right. They may spend substantial time considering and analyzing without acting. They want to fully understand and assess before acting or they believe in chance or luck. They are motivated by phrases such as: consider the following, let's investigate this further, analyze this, we need to understand this, this time we will be lucky. This group can be identified through their use of long, complex sentences or incomplete sentences, use of the passive voice and nominalizations (the noun form of a verb, e.g., *communication* rather than *communicate*), use of conditionals (would, should, could, might, may). They will also speak in terms of outside forces having a major influence on their lives and relying on luck or the need to understand and analyze before acting. As a parent with a Reactive child, you may wish to give him a defined time to think about or analyze your request and let him know that you expect him to take action after this period. "Take until Tuesday to think about my request, and then we can sit down and discuss your thoughts and put a plan into action."

5. Sameness – Difference
Do your children look for things that are the same or different?

This meta program actually has four different categories. For the purposes of this book, I have grouped them into Sameness and Difference.

Sameness: People in this group want their world to remain the same or to change slowly over time. To motivate these people, point out how things have not changed, that they are still doing the same or similar type of activities. Use phrases such as: same as, similar to, in common, as you always do, like before, same except, gradual improvement. If your children fall in this group and you are moving to a new home, point out those things that will be the same or similar – they will have their own rooms and furniture, the family will eat breakfast and supper together, they can invite their friends over from their former neighborhood. Children with a preference for sameness will learn best by noticing how the new ideas or information are similar to what they already know and how each new idea builds on the last. Your role is to emphasize areas of agreement and how this is simply a continuity of previous ideas or information.

Difference: Change is a way of life for people in this group. They expect or will orchestrate major change every one to three years. Motivating words include: new, fresh, totally different, completely changed, radical idea. No matter how much things remain the same, point out all the things that are different, how things are constantly changing, and if feasible get them involved in planning and leading changes within the family. Children with a preference for difference will learn best by seeing how the new ideas or information are different from what they already know and will notice what is missing or does not fit. Your role is to show that what they are learning is new and unique. They will enjoy exercises to spot what is different, what is missing and how things have changed. Sometimes people in this group are referred to as *mismatchers*. They can be the source of a great deal of frustration for a person with a preference for sameness because they easily spot differences/mismatches and enjoy doing things differently.

Combinations of meta programs

I have presented each of the traits separately. To get greater insight, look at various combinations. For example, if your children want to become entrepreneurs, what meta programs would you help them develop? I suggest: Toward, Internal, Options, Proactive and Differences. You can help your children develop these traits by discussing the meta programs, helping them to view the world through these perspectives and setting up rewards and feedback that supports these attributes. In addition, children who understand and have access to both ends of the spectrum for each meta program will be even more successful.

Coaching your children to achieve a desired outcome

The meta programs can be used to provide different contexts for conversation in which to explore and support your children in making changes in their lives or achieving a desired outcome. The following process, which can be as short as an hour or unfold over a longer period – a week or more, has been adapted from The Axes of Change by NLP trainer and author Michael Hall (*Coaching Conversations: For Transformational Change*, Neuro-Semantic Publications, 2005). Some concepts and techniques are presented that are explained later in this book.

Situation: Your child has identified a possible change and at this time is not fully committed to carrying it out. She has asked you for assistance.

1. **Establish an environment of trust and safety.** Let your child know that you're there to support her, that you'll ask her a number of questions – some easy, others not so easy. Assure her that she is in control of the process and is the one who will decide when and how to proceed with the possible change.

2. **Identify the possible change.** "What change do you want to make, and haven't fully committed to making?"

3. **Establish motivation to change.** Determine and enhance her motivation by asking questions from an Away From (Challenger) and a Toward (Awakener) perspective.
   - As a Challenger, with rapport, challenge her concept of reality, explore what she would like to avoid or fix. If she is reluctant to make changes, you may wish to ask questions such as "If you didn't make this change, what would your life be like in five or ten years from now?"
   - As an Awakener, with sincere curiosity, explore possibilities with her. Encourage her to really stretch her thoughts about what might be possible.

4. **Establish commitment to change.** Encourage her to make a firm commitment by asking questions from a Reflective (Prober) and a Proactive (Provoker) perspective.

   - As a Prober, coming from curiosity and non-judgment, use the *precision model* to assist her in gaining clarity on what she would like to achieve and what this will lead to. If relevant, determine what is holding her back.
   - As a Provoker, in a playful spirit, encourage her to make a firm commitment to make the change. If appropriate, you may wish to be bold and ask, "What are you waiting for?" "Are you big enough to get this done?"

   Continue interchanging the roles of Challenger, Awakener, Prober and Provoker until your child is clear on what she wants to do and makes a firm commitment to do so.

5. **Create a plan.** Assist her with determining how she will achieve the change by asking questions from an Options (Co-Creator) and a Procedures (Actualizer) perspective.

   - As a Co-Creator, from a state of playfulness and creation, explore with her: what has she done so far, what are her next steps, are there alternative ways, what other strategies are possible, can she contact someone who has done something like this before?
   - As an Actualizer, from a state of practicality, assist her in determining the first and subsequent steps. Use the precision model to determine who will be involved, what specifically will be achieved, when and where?

6. **Identify milestones.** Assist her in determining how she will know if she is making progress (reaching milestones) or if corrective action will be required from an Internal (Assessor) and External (Observer) perspective.

   - Taking an Assessor perspective, with genuine curiosity, have her notice what personal standards must be satisfied and how she will know inside that she is making progress.
   - As an Observer, help her become aware of what she needs to see, hear, touch, understand (and if relevant, smell or taste) to know that she is on course or if corrective action is required.

   Continue interchanging the roles of Co-Creator, Actualizer, Assessor and Observer until your child is clear on her plan and how she will measure progress. Ensure your child has prepared her desired outcome using the MASTERY format.

7. **Support your child on her journey.** Once your child has clearly defined her outcome and prepared her plan, reinforce her accomplishment with positive feedback and appropriate rewards. At established review points, assist your child with integrating and feeling good about what she has achieved and will accomplish. Help her with continuing her journey by supporting her from a Sameness (Reinforcer) and a Difference (Tester) perspective.

   - As a Reinforcer, with real excitement and joy, compliment her on her successes, no matter how big or small. "Wow, look at what you've created!" Provide incentives or rewards, if required.
   - As a Tester, with rapport and intention to support, determine what else she could do, how could her vision be better/bigger, what is missing, what would really excite/challenge her. If appropriate you may wish to revisit some of the earlier roles, for example, Awakener, Provoker.

3.5 THE HIDDEN TRAITS THAT INFLUENCE HOW YOU INTERACT WITH OTHERS

The logical levels model provides useful insight on how you interact with others, a context for assisting and understanding change at the individual and family level, and a framework for describing and illustrating the six major parenting roles you perform: caretaker/guide, coach, teacher, mentor, sponsor and awakener. This model was developed by Robert Dilts, based on the neurological levels proposed by anthropologist Gregory Bateson. (Robert Dilts, Changing Belief Systems with NLP, Meta Publications, 1990). The six logical levels, their hierarchy and the questions that assist in defining these levels are presented in Table 1: Logical Levels.

You and your family operate at all of these levels. Depending on the circumstances, some levels are more important than others. For example, if you are crossing a very busy street, paying attention to the Environment and Behavior levels, where you are and what you are doing is more important than focusing on your life's Purpose.

The following scenario provides an overview of how the logical levels work. Notice how the higher levels influence the lower levels.

Assume it is 9:00 a.m. on Saturday and your child is at home (environment level). If he wants to be somewhere else, he must change his behavior. He has many choices: Go for a walk. Drive the car. Start yelling and screaming, with the hope someone will take him somewhere else.

The behavior he selects depends on his (conscious and unconscious) capabilities and strategies. If he is capable of driving a car, going for a drive is certainly a possibility. On the other hand, his strategy may be to have someone do things for him, so yelling and screaming may be a good choice.

TABLE 1: LOGICAL LEVELS

Level	Questions corresponding to logical levels (for individuals or groups)
Spirituality/ Purpose	**Who else?** This can be viewed as your personal or family's connection to a larger system or a higher power. As an individual, possible larger systems are family, social or networking groups. Possible larger systems for your family are your community or culture.
Identity/ Mission	**Who?** Who are you as an individual or family? How do you see yourself as a parent – disciplinarian or guide/mentor? What role does your family carry out? Does it provide a safe and nurturing environment?
Beliefs/ Values	**Why?** Why do you do something? What do you believe in or value? For example, you may believe if given the right support your children can accomplish anything they choose. You and your family may value honesty or respect for your elders.
Capabilities/ Strategies	**How?** How do you go about doing things? As an individual or family, what are your capabilities/skills or plans? For example, are you capable of creating a safe place for children to express themselves, plans for financing your children's education?
Behavior	**What?** What are your individual behaviors? What are the collective behaviors of the family? Do you acknowledge your children when they do a good job? Does your family participate in community events?
Environment	**Where? When? With Whom?** Where, when and with whom do you and your family display your behaviors? What are the external influences and constraints (e.g., community, economy) upon you or your family?

The capability or strategy he chooses will depend on his beliefs and values. If he believes he needs help to do things, a strategy of yelling and screaming is a possibility. If he values independence, this would have encouraged him to learn how to drive.

His beliefs and values are determined by his identity. If he sees himself as a resourceful young man who can do things for himself, it is unlikely he would hold a belief that other family members must do things for him.

His identity is dependent on his purpose in life – the impact that he wishes to have on his friends, family, community and society.

To further illustrate how the higher logical levels influence those below them, recall when you believed in Santa Claus. This belief resulted in capabilities/strategies that gave rise to specific behaviors to ensure Santa brought you the presents you wanted. Then one day you no longer believed in Santa Claus and in a flash you developed new strategies/capabilities and corresponding behaviors to ensure you still had influence over the presents you received.

Using logical levels to explain/understand change

The above examination of logical levels leads to several interesting observations:

1. Short-term versus long-term change: A logical level has significant influence over those levels below it and less influence over those levels above it. Thus, for personal change or change within the family to be long-lasting and sustainable, the change must either be in alignment with the higher logical levels or must be effected at the highest possible logical level.

    Occasionally, people have found that NLP techniques changed an unwanted behavior for a short period. Eventually, however, the original behavior returned. The reason: since the new behavior was not in alignment with the beliefs and values or identity, the higher level would eventually override the lower level.

2. Change within the family: Have you ever been involved in change within a family? What are some of the more common change activities?

    How about assigning new responsibilities? Or perhaps a change in room assignments. These are changes at the level of environment. Do you think they will be long-lasting? Only if the changes are in alignment with the higher logical levels.

    Or perhaps children are informed they must perform in a different way behaviorally, without really being taught *how* to do it – this is the capabilities/strategies level. Unfortunately, this happens far too often. Again, the change will most likely not be long-lasting, because the behavioral level change is not supported at the capabilities/strategies level.

On the other hand, family members will change their behaviors if the change provides them with something they perceive to be valuable. Unfortunately, parents often explain planned family changes only in terms of how they will help the family rather than in terms of direct value for the child.

3. Driven by unconscious influences: Suppose your outcome is to be an active, fully present, contributing member of the family – a behavior level activity. Further, suppose you see yourself as a successful businessperson and unconsciously you value business success and contributing financially to the family far more than physically being present and actively participating with your family. Do you think you will achieve your outcome?

Getting to know another person

Suppose you meet a stranger. What do you know about her? Do you know her purpose? Her mission? Her beliefs and values? Her strategies? No, not without establishing trust and safety, and engaging her in a meaningful conversation on these topics. Without asking questions and allowing her to feel safe, all you will know is what she is doing (behavior) and when, where and with whom (environment) she is doing it. The information about her behaviors and where she is exhibiting these behaviors can give you an indication of her strategies, beliefs/values, etc. Without confirming your insights with her, however, they remain only guesses.

If the order of the logical levels is reversed and environment is put at the top and spirituality/purpose at the bottom, this stranger is like a gigantic iceberg with environment (where, when, with whom) and behavior (what) available for anyone to see, while the other logical levels operate below the surface, out of sight. You'll only get to know this person, or yourself for that matter, if you explore what is below the surface – strategies/capabilities, beliefs/values, etc.

If you do not establish trust and safety and engage those who are important to you in a meaningful conversation at the higher logical levels (what's hidden below the surface), you'll never truly get to know them. In fact, many people have never asked *themselves* these very questions. Thus they amble through life aimlessly without being consciously aware of their beliefs and values, identity or purpose in life. The same can be said about your family – what are the beliefs and values that really drive how your family operates on a daily basis?

Having conversations with another person at the higher logical levels provides you with a more intimate understanding of that person and why they behave in the manner they do. How often do you have a conversation with a family member, yet the topic doesn't go beyond the weather (environment) or what they are doing (behavior)? To discover the true essence of your children, you need to discuss who they see themselves being (identity) or what is important to them about life, future career or relationships (values). To engage in this type of conversation, you need to create a space where each of you feels safe in disclosing your "inner selves."

Aligning logical levels for personal congruence

In NLP, when we talk about *personal congruence*, we often mean an internal alignment among the logical levels. For many of us, the logical levels operate outside of our conscious awareness. Whether we're aware of them or not, they have a significant influence over the quality of our lives.

The following exercise will help you to: 1) Become consciously aware of which factors influence how you live your life. 2) Identify possible conflicts. 3) Recognize possible changes you can make to bring the levels more in alignment and hence achieve a higher level of personal congruence (reduced inner conflict).

First identify a context or larger system in which you participate, for instance, your family. Now answer the following questions. Some people find it easier to answer the Environment questions first, then those for behavior, as they work their way up the logical levels. This is fine, as long as the last pass through the questions goes from Spirituality to Environment.

Spirituality/purpose: For the larger system, what is your vision, purpose or the impact you wish to have?

Identity/mission: Who are you or what role do you play? Does the role fully contribute to achieving your purpose? What do you need to change in order to fully achieve your purpose?

Beliefs/values: What beliefs do you have about yourself, about others, about the world in general? Do these beliefs support you in fulfilling your role? What do you value – in yourself, others, the world in general? Are these values in alignment with your role? Could you take on other beliefs and values that would be more in alignment?

Capabilities/strategies: What capabilities/strategies/action plans do you have? Do you need to develop new capabilities, strategies or action plans? Are they in alignment with each of the above logical levels? If not, what needs to be changed? Perhaps you need to change your capabilities (get more training), or change your strategies or action plans. Or perhaps, given this new information, you need to reassess your purpose, your role or your beliefs and values.

Behavior: What do people really see or experience in your behaviors? Does something need to be changed? What actions will you take to achieve your vision?

Environment: When, where, with whom do you exhibit these behaviors? Are they in alignment with the above logical levels?

This exercise can also be undertaken with a focus on the family with the larger context being contributing to your community.

3.6 OVERVIEW OF THIS CHAPTER

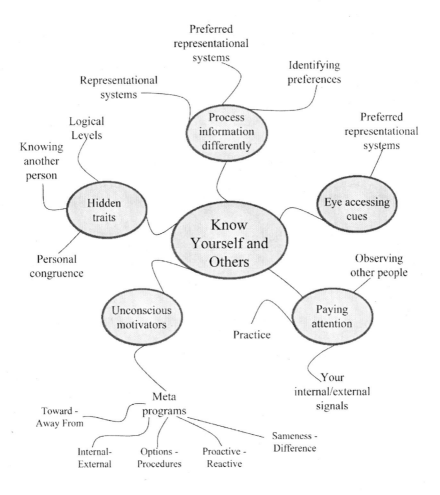

FIGURE 5: MIND MAP OF THIS CHAPTER:
GETTING TO KNOW YOURSELF AND OTHERS

4.

Improving Your Communication

4.1 RAPPORT – ESTABLISHING TRUST AND SAFETY

Rapport is the foundation for any meaningful interaction between two or more people – whether it relates to a conversation with a neighbor, interacting with your children's teachers or providing feedback to your children. Rapport is critical for all you do in business, at home or at play.

Rapport can be described in a number of ways. For me, rapport is about establishing an environment of trust, understanding, respect and safety, which gives all people the freedom to fully express their ideas and concerns and the knowledge that these will be respected by the other person(s). Rapport creates the space for the person to feel listened to and heard; it does not, however, mean that one person must agree with what another says or does. Instead, each person appreciates the other's viewpoint and respects their model of the world.

When you're in rapport with another person, you have the opportunity to enter her world, see things from her perspective, appreciate why she feels the way she does, and arrive at a better understanding of who she is. As a result, the whole relationship is enhanced.

Consider the following:

- Have you noticed how, when people enjoy being with each other, they have a tendency to use the same words and phrases, dress in a similar way or have matching body language?
- Have you observed that people who are not in rapport have differing postures, gestures, voice tonality or don't make eye contact?
- Do you tend to gravitate to other parents with similar aged children? Or if you meet a stranger and discover she has children, does your conversation become more animated as you share common experiences? And as you

discover you have many things in common, do you seem to have more of a connection?

- Have you ever gone to a party or event for which the dress was formal, yet someone arrived dressed very casually? What was your first reaction? Did you feel that they somehow did not belong to the group? Or have you been at a restaurant and everybody at your table has been served their food except you? How did you feel? Uncomfortable, out of place?

The above points illustrate:

- The more you like the other person, the more you want to be like them.
- The more you have in common with another person, the stronger is your bond with them.

Matching and mirroring

The key to establishing rapport is an ability to enter another person's world by assuming a similar state of mind. This is done by becoming more like the other person – by *matching* and *mirroring* their behaviors, including body language, experiences, verbal language and tone of voice. Matching and mirroring are powerful methods of developing an appreciation for how the other person is seeing and experiencing the world.

The terms matching and mirroring are used interchangeably by some NLP practitioners, while others draw the following distinction: When you mirror someone, it is as if you're looking into a mirror. To mirror a person who has raised his right hand, you would raise your left hand – a mirror image. To match this same person, you would raise your right hand – doing exactly the same as this person. I do not draw a significant distinction between matching and mirroring and refer to both of them as matching.

Consider matching body language first, then voice and finally the person's words. Why? Mehrabian and Ferris ("Inference of Attitudes from Nonverbal Communication in Two Channels," *Journal of Counselling Psychology*, Vol. 31, 1967, pp. 248–52) discovered that 55 percent of the impact of a presentation is determined by your body language, 38 percent by your voice and only 7 percent by the content or words you use. The percentages will differ in different contexts; nonetheless, body language and voice tonality have a major impact on your communication and ability to establish rapport.

Body language includes body posture, facial expressions, hand gestures, breathing and eye contact. As a beginner, start by matching one specific behavior and once you are comfortable doing that, match another and so on.

For voice, you can match tonality, speed, volume, rhythm and clarity of speech. All of us can vary aspects of our voice and have a range in which we feel comfortable doing so. If someone speaks much faster than you do and at a rate at which you would not feel comfortable, match this person by speaking a little faster, while staying within a range that is comfortable for you.

For spoken language, match predicates. If your partner is using mainly visual words, you should also use mainly visual words; likewise for auditory, kinesthetic and auditory digital words. To the extent possible, you should also use the same words as the other person. For example, I may say something is "awesome." In your model of the world, you may interpret "awesome" as "outstanding" and use this word when speaking to me. For me, "outstanding" may have a different meaning or evoke a feeling different from "awesome." In this case, you would be mismatching, not matching, my words. If you have identified the other person's meta programs, you can use words that match those meta programs.

Some people find the idea of matching another person uncomfortable; they feel they're trying to fool or take advantage of the other person. To overcome this uneasiness, realize that matching is a natural part of the rapport-building process and that you actually do it unconsciously every day with your close family and friends. Have you ever noticed that if a close friend uses a particular word or sequence of words that soon you too are using them?

As I was listening to the radio the other day, I noticed a good example of unconscious matching. There were two on-air hosts (a man and woman). The man had a very relaxed, calm, gentle nature to him and his co-host behaved in much the same way. That day, the man was replaced by an on-air personality who hosts a hard-rock show. Her demeanor was fast-paced and loud. Interestingly, that day the regular female co-host was also fast-paced and loud, and at first I didn't recognize her voice.

Does matching work?
William Maddux at the INSEAD business school in Fontainebleau, France, explored the effect of matching on 166 students in two role-play experiments – one involved negotiation between job candidates and recruiters and the second between buyers and sellers (*Journal of Experimental Social Psychology*, Vol. 44, p. 461). In both cases, the outcome of negotiations was better for the would-be persuaders when they employed subtle matching. For example, in the buyer-seller experiment, 67 percent of sellers who matched the other person secured a sale, as opposed to 12.5 percent of those who did not.

The critical factors in matching are: be subtle, leave a small delay (two to four seconds) and, if you think your actions have been detected, stop.

Practice matching with family members. It's a valuable skill for them to learn as well. Have fun with it and observe whether they notice what you're doing. Start by matching one specific behavior; once you're comfortable doing that, match another. For friends, notice how often you naturally match their postures, gestures, tone of voice or words. Matching comes naturally; what takes practice is learning how to do it with everyone, not just those with whom you're already in rapport. In time, you'll find matching will become automatic whenever you wish to deepen your rapport with someone.

Experiencing the value of matching

To experience the value of establishing rapport through matching, consider the following two-part exercise. This is a fun exercise you can do with your children. In this example, let's call the two participants Ryan and Sarah.

Part 1. Ryan and Sarah select a topic on which they have a different opinion; for example, one likes broccoli, the other doesn't. Both Ryan and Sarah fully participate in the discussion. As they discuss the topic, Ryan deliberately matches Sarah's body language, voice and choice of words. The conversation continues for about five minutes, after which they assess the quality of their conversation. Often what will happen is that although Ryan and Sarah originally had a difference of opinion, as the exercise proceeds they begin to either explore areas of agreement or find that they have a much better appreciation of the other's point of view.

Part 2. Ryan and Sarah select a topic on which they agree. As they discuss the topic, Sarah deliberately mismatches Ryan's body language, voice and choice of words (this time Ryan does not match Sarah, he simply participates in the discussion). The conversation continues for about five minutes, after which they assess the quality of their conversation. For this part of the exercise, it's not unusual for Ryan to become frustrated with Sarah and not wish to continue with the conversation, even though initially they had both agreed on the topic.

Examples of mismatching are: speaking fast or loud when the other person is speaking slow or softly, sitting differently, standing rather than sitting, not looking at the other person, using different words/predicates.

Using matching with your children

When your children first come home from school or you come home from work, are you busy with or in deep thought about something else? Do you encourage your children to tell you about their experiences at school, while mismatching – standing much taller than them, facing in another direction, getting supper ready or reading the mail or newspaper? Put yourself in their shoes for a minute. How much fun is it to tell your parents about the exciting things at school when they aren't even looking at you and they are so distracted that the best you get from your parents in a monotone voice is "That's nice."

What would happen if you changed your behavior and for the next five to ten minutes fully focused on them and matched their body language, tone of voice (including the excitement in their voices) and their choice of words. That is, what if you really engaged them in a conversation and established a connection? Examples of matching could include: kneeling down to a small child so you're at his eye level, sitting at the kitchen table and having a glass of milk and cookies together, getting down on the floor and building something together as he tells about his day, going outside and throwing a ball to each other, going to his room and looking at the artwork he brought home and discussing where it would look best.

Pacing and leading

Pacing is the process of establishing rapport through matching. Once rapport has been established, *leading* is the process of changing your physiology, tone of voice, or choice of words to assist the other person in favorably changing either his physiology or state. For example, you may have witnessed two people in rapport, pacing their behaviors agreeably. Then, one person changes his body position (leading), followed a few minutes later by the other person changing to this same body position. Why would this be useful? Well, let's assume your child is upset. You can pace his behavior by matching body language, voice and words. Once you have established rapport, you can begin to lead him into a calmer, more resourceful state by gradually changing your physiology and voice tonality to that of a calm, resourceful state. A caution: if your child is angry, match with an intensity less than his level, otherwise you may worsen the situation.

4.2 GAINING A DIFFERENT PERSPECTIVE

Perceptual positions – walking a mile in someone else's shoes

Getting different perspectives on an event or situation provides a more balanced approach to your thinking and subsequent actions. In situations where there is little or no understanding or progress, *perceptual positions* can provide a way of developing new understandings and creating new choices. The ability to experience yourself, your actions and their possible impacts from different perspectives is an essential part of effective communication. These are the four perceptual positions:

- First position: Experiencing the situation from your perspective. What did you see, hear and feel? You think in terms of what is important to you, what you want to achieve.
- Second position: Stepping into the shoes of the other person and experiencing (seeing, hearing and feeling) the situation as if you were that person. To the best of your knowledge and ability, you take on the other person's beliefs/values, attitude, personal history and physiology and think in terms of how

this situation would be interpreted from her perspective. You've heard the expression: "Before criticizing someone, walk a mile in their shoes."

- Third position: Standing back from the situation and experiencing it as if you were a detached observer. In your mind, you are able to see and hear yourself and the other person(s), as if watching strangers on TV. You act as an independent, resourceful third person and observe the interaction – the sequence of words, gestures, and expressions that occur in the communication – free of evaluation or judgment. You think in terms of what observations or advice an independent, uninvolved person would provide to the person who looks and sounds like you.
- Fourth position: Viewing from the perspective of the larger system. If you are a parent having a discussion with your child, the larger system is the family. The fourth position is about ecology as you explore how your actions have an impact on the larger system, including those people who are part of this system and how the system may constrain what you perceive is possible.

All four positions are of equal importance and it is useful, consciously or unconsciously, to cycle through them as you go about your daily activities. Sometimes, however, you remain stuck in one of these positions:

- Someone who lives his life in first position would tend to focus on his own needs rather than the needs of others – a self-centered attitude. Addicts tend to see the world from first position.
- Someone who lives her life primarily in second position is always thinking about the other person at the expense of her own needs. Co-dependents or enablers in a dysfunctional or addiction situation would fit this description.
- Someone who lives in third position is a disconnected observer of life, quite capable of giving himself or others advice, and never putting it into action for himself.
- Someone who lives in fourth position would see all of the group (family) dynamics, see what is necessary to keep the family functioning, and may not be fully aware of her needs.

Improving communication with family members
Sometimes you have noble outcome(s) for yourself and your family, yet your behaviors – the way you communicate – are not in alignment to achieve your outcome(s), and you end up creating something other than what you desire. The following exercise will help you to align your behaviors with your outcome(s).

1. Make yourself comfortable and review in your mind your interactions with key family members from first position. Notice what you see, hear and feel. When finished, break state by looking around the room, standing or stretching your body.

To understand how a person's eyes move, ask the following questions of your children and notice the direction their eyes move – up, down or to the side.

- What was the color of your bedroom walls when you were ten years old?
- What will you look like in ten years?
- What does your favorite music sound like?
- What would your voice sound like if you had marbles in your mouth?
- When you talk to yourself, what type of voice do you use?
- What does it feel like to be in a nice, warm bath?

Did you notice their eyes had a tendency to look up for the first two questions, to the side for the next two questions and down for the last two questions? In general, if they are forming a picture in their mind, their eyes will tend to go up to the left or the right; for sounds laterally to the left or right; and down to the left or right for feelings or when they talk to themselves.

More specifically, if they are right-handed, you may have noticed the following (for people who are left-handed, exchange left and right in the following text):

- Question 1 – eyes up and to their left. This is a question about something they have seen before; hence, they remembered it – visual remembered (V^R).

- Question 2 – eyes up and to their right. This is a question about something they have not seen before; hence, they constructed this picture – visual constructed (V^C).

- Question 3 – eyes on the horizontal plane to their left. This is a question about something they have heard before – auditory remembered (A^R).

- Question 4 – eyes on the horizontal plane to their right. This is a question about something they have not heard before – auditory constructed (A^C).

- Question 5 – eyes down and to their left. This is a question about their self-talk – auditory digital (A_d).

- Question 6 – eyes down and to their right. This is a question about their feelings – kinesthetic (K).

Note: The following picture summarizes the eye patterns for a right-handed person as *you look at them* – please note this distinction. These patterns are fairly consistent across all races. For many left-handed people, the chart is reversed (a mirror image).

Looking at the other person

FIGURE 4: EYE PATTERN CHART

If you would like to have some fun with members of your family, here are some other questions you can take turns asking one another – or you can make up your own.

Visual remembered
- What is the color of the shirt you wore yesterday?
- Which of your friends has the shortest hair?

Visual constructed
- What would your room look like if it were painted yellow with big purple circles?
- Imagine the top half of a tiger on the bottom half of an elephant.

Auditory remembered
- What does your best friend's voice sound like?
- Which is louder, your doorbell or your telephone?

Auditory constructed
- What will your voice sound like in ten years?
- What would it sound like if you played your two favorite pieces of music at the same time?

2. From second position – to the best of your ability – take on the beliefs/ values and physiology for each key family member (one at a time and break state each time you access a different family member). Notice from their perspectives how they perceive your behaviors. Is this what you had intended to achieve? Are your actions improving your communication with family members and moving you closer to achieving your outcome(s)?

3. From third position, taking a fully independent perspective, observe the interaction between you and key family members. Do these observations suggest possible changes you could make in your behaviors to improve your communication and move you closer to achieving your outcome(s)? Break state.

4. From fourth position, notice the impact your actions have on the family at this time. Now, fast forward one, five or ten years into the future and notice the potential future impact of your behaviors. Is this what you planned to achieve? Do these observations suggest possible changes in your behaviors?

5. Taking into account the information you obtained from steps two through four, are there changes you would like to make in your behaviors to improve your communication with family members? If the answer is yes, make these changes and repeat steps one through four with these new behaviors in mind. Continue with the above steps until your behaviors are in alignment with your outcome(s).

This exercise can be used to assist your child in getting different perspectives on his behaviors if he is having difficulty with a friend, his teachers or other family members.

I often use a similar exercise in public presentations. At one event, as I finished leading those in attendance through the exercise, a young lady quickly left the room. She returned about twenty minutes later and, at the next break, approached me and apologized for leaving the room the way she had. She explained that about two weeks earlier, she'd had a major fight with her roommate and longtime close friend that resulted in her moving out. The two of them had not spoken to one another since. Now, however, as a result of doing the exercise, she realized how she could have handled the situation differently and left the room to telephone her friend. After the positive outcome of this new conversation, she was planning to move back in with her friend that very evening.

Exercises with perceptual positions can be used to learn from an event in the past, an event in the present (to gain an appreciation of how you are doing and whether you should take corrective action) or for a future event (for instance, to plan a fun day with your family).

Quadrants – different perspectives on an issue

Often an issue/problem will limit what is possible or stop you from taking action because you are looking at it from only one perspective. *Cartesian quadrants*, based on the Cartesian co-ordinate system in mathematics, provide an opportunity to explore the issue from four different perspectives.

The process:

1. Be fully open to explore your issue and proposed course of action from different directions.

2. Relax and ask yourself the following questions one at a time, in the order indicated. Take time to fully explore the questions and obtain answers for both the short and long term. If one or more of the questions seems confusing when you first attempt to answer it, relax and allow answers to come to you.

3. What wouldn't happen if you did?	1. What would happen if you did?
4. What wouldn't happen if you didn't?	2. What would happen if you didn't?

For example, if you have an issue about the amount of time you spend with your family, you may wish to consider the following four questions:

- What would happen if I spent more time with my family?
- What would happen if I didn't spend more time with my family?
- What wouldn't happen if I spent more time with my family?
- What wouldn't happen if I didn't spend more time with my family?

You can be assured that once you have fully considered each of these questions, you'll have more clarity on your choices and possible courses of action.

More specific or more general

Would it be useful to have a process that assists you or your children with:

- Finding common areas of agreement in a negotiation or argument?
- Overcoming a feeling of being overwhelmed with an activity?
- Increasing your excitement or interest in accomplishing a task?
- Quickly and easily thinking laterally to get a different perspective on a problem or issue or to uncover other possible solutions?

Chunking is an NLP process that will do just that. For example, sometimes our conversation with a family member is not as effective as we would like because we have been either too abstract/vague or provided too much detail. In the former, smaller chunks (more detail) of information are required (called *chunking down*), while in the latter larger chunks (bigger picture) of information would be more appropriate (*chunking up*).

The process

To chunk up on a piece of information, use one or more of the following questions:

- What is this an example of?
- What is this a part of?
- What is the intention or purpose?

To illustrate the concept with an easy example, let's begin with a library building. Examples of chunking up from library building would be:

- Buildings (a library building is an example of many kinds of buildings).
- A city block (the library building forms part of a city block).
- A city's library system (the library building is part of this system).
- A system that provides a means for people to undertake research.

If we follow the path of a city block, we can then chunk up to a city, then to a province or state, then to a country, and so on.

To chunk down, use one or more of the following questions:

- What is an example of this?
- What is a component/part of this?
- What/who/where specifically?

Examples of chunking down or being more specific on a library building are:

- A library building in the city of Seattle.
- A library building built in the 1950s.
- The third floor of the library building.
- A shelf of books in the library building.

If we follow the path of a shelf of books, we can continue chunking down – getting more specific – to children's books, books written by Dr. Seuss, a specific Dr. Seuss book, then a particular chapter and so on.

The above are just a few examples. Depending on your particular focus or thought pattern, you may come up with many different examples. In a real situation, the path you follow will be determined by the context and your intention.

How and when can you use chunking?

When supporting your child, this simple concept of chunking has many varied and useful applications:

- Discover the positive intention behind a behavior or an appropriate context for a behavior. You can chunk up or down on the logical levels. For example, if your child is exhibiting a certain behavior, you may choose to become curious and chunk up by asking yourself what strategy is he using or what his intention is (e.g., what value or belief is being satisfied?). To chunk down on a specific behavior, you may become curious as to where, when or with whom (environment level) it is a useful activity.

- Improve negotiation. Far too often in negotiation, we continue to explore solutions at a level of thought at which we do not agree. The key is to chunk up until you and your child agree and then to chunk back down to the details only as fast as you both maintain agreement. Often in negotiation we guess what the other person wants, and often our guess is off the mark.

During one NLP practitioner training session, we were reviewing material from previous days and how the students could use it. One woman from out of town described how she had called her husband and asked him what he wanted to do upon her return. He immediately suggested, "Let's go to the cottage for the weekend." Having been away from home for over a week, she did not relish the idea of repacking immediately and going to the cottage. Recalling the chunking process, she asked him in a supportive tone, "You would like to go to the cottage – for what purpose?" His answer was, "To spend time with you." This approach opened up many more options for her to pursue that would meet her husband's need and that would also be acceptable to her. While I don't remember what they decided to do, I do recall that she was very pleased and said it avoided a possible troublesome argument.

- Create a passion. By chunking up and down, you can assist your child with generating excitement, motivation and passion for achieving his outcome, while adjusting it to a manageable size.

   o Overcoming a lack of interest. Why do people get bored? Often because what they are doing does not excite them. They are mired in the details. If your child has a task to complete and he is not excited about it, assist him to explore the question, "What is the purpose of this task?" or "What can you gain by completing this task?" His first reply or two may not be too motivating. Keep at it and eventually he will identify a motivating reason. This is an example of chunking up. Pursuing an activity and not knowing the larger purpose can be demotivating.

   o Addressing overwhelmed feelings. Feelings of being overwhelmed can occur if the chunk size is too large. Assist your child with chunking down and being more specific, potentially identifying smaller steps, or being more realistic. After all, how do you eat an elephant? One bite at a time! If your child feels overwhelmed or does not know where to start, assist him in chunking down to identify specific manageable tasks.

• Create rapport and improve your ability to communicate. If your child is more comfortable with details and you would like her to gain an appreciation for the bigger picture, first chunk down to her level of detail, matching her chunk size, to establish rapport and to show her you understand her view. Then gradually increase the chunk size to assist her in gaining an understanding of the larger picture. In a similar manner, if your child is stuck in the "big picture" and doesn't know what to do next, you can assist her in chunking down to identify the steps necessary to move toward her outcome.

• Think laterally. We're often encouraged to think laterally. While this is not always easy to do, it can be if you use chunking. To think laterally, first chunk up, then chunk down. For example, suppose you have to take your child to an event and your car is not available. To identify alternatives, first chunk up, for instance, what is your car an example of? One possible chunk up is a mode of transportation. Next, by chunking down, you can easily identify many different modes of transportation that are on the same level as car – for example, bicycle, bus, train, airplane, horse or walking. That is, you can easily think beyond the norm and potentially come up with an innovative solution that meets your needs.

• Brainstorming. Similar to thinking laterally, the first step in a brainstorming session is to chunk up to gain clarity on the overall outcome and then from this perspective chunk down to explore ideas/steps that satisfy this outcome.

4.3 THE INNER CONVERSATION

At a deep level of thought, a speaker has complete knowledge of what he wishes to communicate to someone else. This is called the *deep structure* and operates at an unconscious level. To be efficient in his communication, the speaker unconsciously deletes, generalizes, limits or distorts his inner thoughts based on his beliefs and values, memories, decisions, strategies and what he wants you to hear. *Surface structure* is whatever he communicates to other people (verbally, written, voice tonality and body language) or to himself (his internal dialogue). What is finally communicated – the surface structure – is only a small subset of the original thought; it may be ambiguous or confusing and lead to miscommunication.

To illustrate deep structure and surface structure and why it is important to be aware of the distinction, consider the following situation. Your child walks into the room and before he says a word and often in a blink of an eye, his inner thoughts – his deep structure – are unconsciously filtered through his model of the world (i.e., his beliefs and values; what he feels he can and cannot say to you). He then says, "My friends don't like me." This single statement reveals only the surface structure of his communication. You filter what he has said through your own beliefs and values, memories and decisions – all those experiences you had as a child – process at your deep structure of thought, then filter this conclusion through what you believe you can say to your child and your assessment (guess) of what is going on in his life. All this occurs in a heartbeat. On this basis, you may then say (surface structure) something such as "I know exactly what you are going through; here is what I did when I was your age." Your advice may be most appropriate for you and most inappropriate for your child, as you have no real understanding of what he meant by "My friends don't like me." As a result, he may not feel understood and next time seek advice and support elsewhere.

To be an effective parent, you need to become curious about what your child said, establish rapport and ask questions that will help both of you gain a better appreciation of his deep structure – what's really going on inside of him. Once you both have this clarity, you're in a better position to provide advice. What often happens is that when your child finally becomes clear on the issue and how to resolve it, he no longer needs your advice, simply your continued support and curiosity. You provide valuable support in helping him discover, through proper questioning and use of language, the path from his surface structure to his deep structure.

A trail to the inner conversation

To make sense of what another person says, you must accept or presume certain information or relationships to be true. These assumptions are called *linguistic presuppositions*, which are different from the NLP presuppositions presented in Chapter 2.

A linguistic presupposition is something that is overtly expressed in the body of the statement itself, which must be presupposed or accepted in order for the sentence or utterance to make sense. It is an inference that can be made from the structure of language that provides a path from the words a person expresses (the surface structure) to what is actually going on inside that person (their inner feelings, thoughts, memories, beliefs and values, often at an unconscious level – the deep structure). Linguistic presuppositions allow for the internal universe of the speaker to be revealed, and thus presumed by the listener from the words that the person is using. Although the information a person reveals through speech may not necessarily be accurate or correct, it will nonetheless reveal what he holds to be true in his model of the world. As the listener gains an understanding of the internal representations of the speaker, she can use different sentence structures or a change in words to offer the speaker alternative internal representations for consideration – thus potentially assisting the speaker in expanding or loosening his model of the world.

Understanding through what is presupposed by your child's choice of words or behavior can provide valuable information to support him on his journey to adulthood.

Presuppositions or a mind read?
As the receiver of a communication, it is crucial to distinguish between what is presupposed in a communication and what you superimpose or assume based on your interpretation of the communication through your filters – your history, beliefs and values. How often have you been in a conversation with someone and made an assumption about what they were saying, only to find out that you had guessed wrong! These inferences, deductions or conjectures that you create on the basis of how you see the world are called *mind reads*.

For example, consider the following sentence: "Ivan left town yesterday after causing a great deal of suffering." Which of the following are presuppositions and which are mind reads?

- There is a person called Ivan.
- Ivan will return and cause more suffering.
- Ivan physically hurt someone.

I was being tricky here – they are all mind reads! Ivan could be many different things – a person, a dog, a hurricane. There is nothing in the sentence that presupposes that Ivan will return. Ivan caused suffering, but we do not know if it was physical or emotional suffering. Did you identify them all as mind reads or did you make assumptions based on your model of the world?

More examples:
Read the following sentence and then decide what is presupposed: "My partner's parents treat my children differently because they're handicapped." I have a partner – yes; my partner has parents – yes; I have children – yes; my children are treated differently – yes; my children are handicapped – mind read. It may be my partner's parents who are handicapped.

Consider the following: "My life is a mess." Does this presuppose that the speaker has an understanding of what her life would be like if it were not a mess? Yes. You can only know whether something is hot if you have an understanding of what "not hot" (cold) is like. Instead of imposing your model of "not mess" on the speaker, you need to become curious and discover what she means internally by a "mess" and then how, from her perspective, her life could be different.

When you read the following, what do you think of? "When did your children first beat you?" Did you think of beating in the context of physical violence or in the competitive sense of winning at a sport or game, or something else? These are mind reads. From the information provided, you cannot know what "beat" means.

Using linguistic presuppositions

You can use linguistic presuppositions to assist your listener in gaining a different perspective on a problem or the world in general. To do this, you need to be aware of the presuppositions that you use in everyday language; they can have a significant impact on the listener. For example, after my father passed away, many well-intentioned people said things such as "I know you're sad at the loss of your father." To make sense of this sentence, I had to accept the speaker's presupposition of "being sad." What do you think was the potential impact on my emotional state? Now consider the sentence: "I know you'll find the strength to cope with the loss of your father." Would this not put me in a different state of mind?

To gain a better perspective on the power of linguistic presuppositions, consider the following examples:

1. "Do you want to work on your school project today or tomorrow?" The main presupposition, or what the listener must accept to make sense of the sentence, is that he will work on his school project. Regarding when, he may have many options from which to choose. However, if he accepts the other presuppositions in the sentence, his choices are limited to "today" or "tomorrow." This is called a *double bind*.

   A double bind you can use with young children (be careful of overusing it, because it will lose its effect) is, "Would you like to go to bed now or after your favorite TV show?" If you planned for them to go to bed after their favorite TV show, you have given away nothing and, by framing this as a question, provided them with the illusion they have choice. Regardless of which specified time your children select, they have committed themselves to going to bed.

2. "Don't resolve this math problem too fast." A presupposition is that it is possible to resolve the problem and the only real question is the speed at which it will be resolved.

3. "After you've finished your homework, you'll notice how easy it is to solve similar problems." Two possible presuppositions are: 1) the homework will be finished, and 2) it's easy to solve similar problems.

4. "Do you want to let your friends know where they can contact you before you leave the property?" My eldest son studied police foundations in college. Some aspects of NLP, in particular linguistic presuppositions, were included in his studies. This sentence was an example used in class. Notice what is presupposed – the listener will leave the property. Saying it in this way is more effective than simply saying, "You are leaving the property." It implies choice, yet the choice is not about leaving the property.

5. "What do you plan to accomplish today?" This question is simple, direct and focuses the listener's attention on the fact that he *will* accomplish something today.

6. "Tell me about this small problem." Your child may come to you with a problem she sees as being huge. You can begin by acknowledging that she sees it as a huge problem – matching, thus establishing rapport. After a while, you begin to refer to it simply as a problem. As the conversation proceeds (over a period of time), you may refer to it as a small problem. Notice what has happened: if you have rapport with your child, you have helped her take her problem from being huge to small – something she can handle. And if eventually you can state it as a problem she *used to have*, it is now a problem in the past.

For linguistic presuppositions to be effective, they must be accepted by the listener's unconscious mind. Obviously, rapport and the listener having a sense of safety are essential to this activity, as is the case for any change-related activity.

The above linguistic presuppositions support the development of the listener. And how many times do you say something that actually plants a negative suggestion. "If you don't do your homework, you will amount to nothing." "Watching TV means you're lazy." "You may not realize it now, but you will have difficulty later in your life." "Don't be so stupid." It is often said that for every positive comment, children hear ten negative comments. If as a child, you lived in this type of environment, what mental models did you form about yourself and the world around you?

4.4 GAINING CLARITY WITH QUESTIONS

When coaching individuals or families, I prefer to ask questions rather than suggest to them what they should do. I believe that at some level of consciousness, we all know what we need to do to achieve our outcomes; we just need someone to assist us in discovering how to begin and what direction to take. If I tell you what I think you should do, my suggestion will be tainted with my model of the world, and I am encouraging you to be at effect rather than at cause. If I were to create a space for you to feel safe exploring your inner thoughts, and then ask you questions that assist you in discovering what is true for you, you would then be at cause for how your life unfolds.

Good questioning skills are invaluable for parents and provide a way to assist your children in moving from the surface structure of their communication to an understanding of their deep structure – their unconscious beliefs, values and decisions. A good set of questions provides a means to gather additional information and offers the potential of clarifying meanings, identifying limitations and opening up choices. An appropriate question asked with rapport can assist your children in exploring other possibilities and interpretations, with the potential to change how they see their circumstances. This is not about finding the right answers but about aiding you and your children in gaining a better understanding of their model of the world.

Fritz Perls (Gestalt therapy) and Virginia Satir (family therapy) were two very successful therapists who obtained extraordinary results with their clients by having them be more specific in what they expressed. That is, by using certain types of questions to gather information, they were able to gain an understanding of their clients' deep structures and thus support them in making significant changes. John Grinder and Richard Bandler, the two co-founders of NLP, modeled these two experts and observed that in moving from the deep structure to the surface structure, people unconsciously:

- Delete: You present only a part of the information that is available at the deep structure.
- Generalize: You make general statements about what you believe and how you perceive others and the world. You ignore possible exceptions or special conditions.
- Distort: You may choose to oversimplify or fantasize about what is possible or what has happened.

To recover the information missing as a result of deleting, generalizing and distorting, Grinder and Bandler identified twelve different patterns with corresponding questions and called this the *meta model*. The meta model is about being more specific – chunking down – to get a better understanding of the person's model of the world. All human communication has the potential to be ambiguous, which can lead to problems. The purpose of the questions is to cut through this ambiguity to access the missing information for both the speaker and the listener. The goal is to gain a better understanding of the speaker's deep structure and make better sense of the communication.

Although based on the work of two therapists, the meta model has much wider application – wherever two or more people are engaged in communicating – whether at work, at play, within the family or in personal relations.

Precision model

John Grinder and Michael McMaster (*Precision: A New Approach to Communication: How to Get the Information You Need to Get Results*, Grinder, DeLozier & Associates, 1994) developed the precision model, a subset of the meta model questions, for gathering information in a business environment. This model is equally useful and most applicable in situations faced by parents.

Once mastered, the precision model is a powerful and useful tool. However, it does take practice to master the questioning process. It must be undertaken with a high degree of rapport – your children must feel safe and not pressured – and used with moderation. Before asking any of my clients, students or family members meta or precision model questions, I make sure that they are comfortable in my presence and have a feeling of security. I often start with the following: "May I ask you a question?" If they respond negatively, I do not pursue it. Instead, I listen to the presuppositions and metaphors in their choice of words to get a clearer understanding of their model of the world.

As a first step in using the precision model, identify the patterns in your own conversations and practice developing the questions that recover the lost information. You may wish to write a few paragraphs about your career, your family or your views of life. Then identify the precision model patterns and corresponding questions. Make sure you honestly answer these questions and notice if new understandings or possibilities are opened up.

Precision model examples

Lack of clarity on who or what

The person(s), object or result to which the statement refers is unspecified or not clear.

Words that indicate this situation are: we, they, friends, teachers, school, people.

Example	Questions to recover lost information
He didn't like the picture on my book.	Who specifically? What picture? Which book?

Lack of clarity on the action

In this case, it is not clear how something was or will be done.

Example	Questions to recover lost information
I improved my study habits.	How specifically did you improve your study habits?

| I need to improve my study habits. | How specifically are you going to improve your study habits? |

Comparison is not obvious

Although a comparison is made, what is being compared is unclear. The sentence will often contain words such as: good, bad, better, best, worst, more, less, most, least, few, improved, great, newer.

Example	Questions to recover lost information
My room is cleaner.	Compared to what?
I did a better job.	Compared to what?
This is a great movie.	Compared to what?
This soap is new and improved.	Compared to what?

Generalization

Here a specific experience is generalized beyond what is fact. Words that indicate this are: all, everyone, nobody, every, never, always. To address generalizations, emphasize the generalization or provide a counter example.

Example	Questions to recover lost information
All parents let their kids attend this show.	All parents? Frank's parents?
Nobody likes me.	Nobody? What about your friend [ ]?
I never get credit for cleaning my room.	Did I not praise you for doing that last week?

Limitations

Limitations are statements that are tied to your or other people's rules or requests that restrict what's possible. Words that indicate this are: can/can't, possible/impossible, should/shouldn't, must/mustn't, have to, need to, necessary.

Example	Questions to recover lost information
I can't get my homework done on time.	What stops you?
We shouldn't do that.	What would happen if we did?
I need to stay after school.	What would happen if you didn't?

Ask "How?" rather than "Why?"

Notice that none of the questions in the precision model begins with "why." When you ask someone a "why" question, often they feel they have to defend what they have said or done, making excuses or rationalizing their behavior. This provides little potential for resolving the issue. Asking "how" gives you an understanding of the process and "how" the problem arose and thus more information and understanding; for example, "How has this become a problem for you?"

4.5 COMMUNICATING WITH YOUR UNCONSCIOUS MIND

The precision model assists you in being more specific or precise about your problem; as a result, you begin to discover (at a conscious level) possible resources or solutions to the problem. And your unconscious mind plays a different and mutually supportive role with your conscious mind in how you perceive and live your life.

Conscious and unconscious minds

George Miller ("The Magic Number Seven, Plus or Minus Two," *The Psychological Review*, 1956, Vol. 63, pp. 81–97) reasoned that the conscious mind is able to keep track of seven plus or minus two chunks of information at a time. Your conscious mind is the part that analyzes, criticizes and thinks logically during the day, then rests at night.

You form habits by consciously learning several small chunks of information, and gradually combining these into increasing larger chunks until, at some point, they become a way of life and you simply do them unconsciously. Thus, your conscious mind is free to become aware of other new information. Remember when you first learned how to drive a car? Where was your attention? Now you can drive a car, be aware of the traffic around you and talk with your passengers in safety, since these behaviors are now unconscious or habitual.

To remember what you have learned, you can consciously call up several large chunks (seven plus or minus two) of information from your unconscious mind. Then, as you become increasingly specific within each succeeding chunk size, you can request more specific information from your unconscious mind.

Your unconscious mind is a major bio-processor, working twenty-four hours a day, that looks after all your bodily functions, is the storehouse for all your habits, decisions, beliefs, past memories and other information you have acquired. It is where your wisdom, creativity and intuitive problem-solving capabilities live. Your unconscious mind is continuously receiving and processing information. Remember earlier I said that it has access to four billion bits of information in any given moment, while your conscious mind can only process two thousand of those bits in seven plus or minus two chunks.

Understanding how the unconscious mind works and develops is important to maximizing positive programming ("I can do whatever I choose") of yourselves and your children and avoiding any negative programming ("I'm stupid").

Brainwaves

Your brain generates electrical signals or brainwaves, which can be measured by an electroencephalograph (EEG). The type of brainwave that your brain emits indicates if you are processing more with your unconscious mind or your conscious mind. Not only that, you can influence the type of brainwave activity you have and hence influence if you are relaxed, creative, more easily influenced by suggestions or able to access accelerated learning capabilities.

Brainwaves are divided into four predominant speed ranges or patterns (cycles per second or hertz [Hz]): delta, theta, alpha and beta. Each type of brainwave plays a critical role in your mental development during childhood. For adults, they play an important role in maintaining your health and vitality. Your brain can be functioning in more than one brainwave state concurrently; however, there are specific times when one state will dominate.

Delta

Delta exhibits the longest and slowest brainwave at 0.5 – 4 Hz. It is the dominant brainwave of infants (from birth to twenty-four months) – awake, nursing or asleep. In adults it occurs during periods of deep sleep and very deep relaxation. There are no feelings or emotions in this state. Your body is healing itself, producing vital hormones such as HGH (human growth hormone, a key element in anti-aging), gaining a sense of well-being and longevity and resetting internal clocks.

Accelerated language retention occurs at this level. If your children are in this age range, engage them in conversation, even if they are not fully capable of responding.

Theta

Children's brainwaves begin to accelerate between the ages of two and six into the faster theta state (4 – 8 Hz), which explains their rich imagination and creativity at this age. In adults, you experience this state as you drift into sleep and just as you wake up. Theta also occurs when you are dreaming, in deep hypnosis, meditating or "in the zone" in sports.

Much of your unconscious potential occurs at this level, with your unconscious mind being totally dominant. This level provides greater access to creativity, insights and intuition. Under hypnosis, many people go into hypnoanaesthesia – so deeply relaxed that surgeries can occur with sensation but without pain.

Studies show that 50 percent of a child's brain capacity is developed in the first five or six years of life. Parents with younger children are encouraged to support their children in exploring what's possible and exposing them to situations and toys that stimulate their creative juices. Speaking slowly in a soft, gentle tone of voice with gentle background music can assist children of all ages to access this state.

Alpha
From six to twelve years of age, children's brainwaves accelerate to the alpha state (8 – 13 Hz).

This level also occurs when we meditate, daydream or enter the lighter states of hypnosis or highway hypnosis – a mental state in which you drive a vehicle, responding to external events in the expected manner, and arrive at your destination with no recollection of having done so. In this mental state, your mind is relaxed yet alert. This is a state of accelerated learning, passive awareness and physical and mental relaxation. Many researchers believe you store information most effectively in your long-term memory when you are in a relaxed yet alert state. Emotional sensations in the alpha state include a sense of well-being, pleasure and tranquility.

Your unconscious mind is still in the forefront and your conscious mind is not yet dominant. Your unconscious mind does not distinguish between what you imagine or actually experience. It simply does what it is told, shown or imagined until it becomes a habit. Thus suggestions (hypnotic or otherwise) can have powerful effects in the alpha, theta (what are you saying to yourself just as you begin to fall asleep?) and delta brainwave states. Be aware of the suggestions you're giving your children that will have an effect on their adult life. Are you suggesting to your children that the world is full of opportunity or that it is a scary place? Hearing messages such as "you are stupid or bad" can create beliefs that may last a lifetime. Encourage your children to dream about what's possible.

To access this state, practice meditation or self-hypnosis. Or learn to breathe in a relaxed manner – slowly inhale a normal amount of air through your nose, filling your lower lungs, then your upper lungs. Exhale slowly and easily.

Beta
At age twelve, children's dominant brainwaves begin to accelerate to beta (13 – 30 Hz) – the most common form of brainwaves. This is the adult state of eyes open, fully alert, focused on what is around us. Beta brainwaves are present during mental thought and activity. The initial effort to understand something or address a problem happens in this state, while the alpha state is very effective

for consolidating information. Beta is the state in which you deal with the day-to-day solving of life's issues. Emotional sensations in this state include anger, worry, fear, anxiety, tension, surprise, excitement and hunger. Here your conscious mind is dominant.

From age twelve on, emotional sensations will be experienced, potentially for the first time. Help your children work through these emotions in a healthy, resourceful and safe manner. Support your children in recognizing, addressing and analyzing their problems.

The Milton model – trance

Usually, when a person is having problems, it's because she has run out of conscious resources. She doesn't know what to do, what she needs or how to access her resources. Trance (hypnosis) bypasses the conscious mind and makes the resources of the unconscious mind available. Trance is not a passive state, nor are you under another's influence. Most significant and long-lasting change takes place at the unconscious level. Each of us has a useful personal history, filled with experiences, knowledge and resources that can be drawn upon, if only we knew how to tap into them.

The Milton model was developed by observing and modeling Milton Erickson, who was generally regarded as the foremost hypnotherapist of his time. He worked with trance and cleverly structured sentences full of vague meanings to help his clients discover how to address their problems and to realize that they already had the necessary coping resources within them. The basis of Erickson's success was his sensory acuity, his ability to read nonverbal behavior, his ability to establish rapport with his clients, his skill with language patterns and his positive beliefs about his clients. Erickson made great use of embedded suggestions, metaphors, anchoring, reframing and submodalities – topics that are covered in this book.

The topic of trance and hypnosis is vast. This section presents three of the language patterns used by Milton Erickson that you can easily use with your children. Delivering these patterns with rapport, while speaking slowly in a soft, gentle tone of voice, you can subtly influence another's thoughts at the unconscious level. These patterns are not limited to trance or personal change work. You will come across each of these patterns in everyday speech. (For more information on hypnosis, the Milton model and other hypnotic techniques, see *Hypnosis: A Comprehensive Guide* by Tad James, The Cromwell Press, 2000.)

Double bind: Invites choice within a larger context of "no choice."

"Do you want to begin now or later?" "Do you want to finish your homework before or after lunch?"

Embedded commands: This is a command that forms part of a larger sentence. In writing, it is marked by the use of italics, and in speech, it is marked by a subtle change in voice tonality or body language that is picked up by the reader's or listener's unconscious.

"I will not suggest to you that *change is easy.*" "You can *learn* this material *easily.*" "Do you think you should *tell your friends about this book.*" In the latter case, notice the sentence has the structure of a question and the embedded command is delivered with the tonality or syntax of a statement or command.

Tag question: Designed to soften resistance or ratify agreement, a tag question follows a more direct, emphatic statement or question. It is used to ensure that the listener has or will actually manifest the implied action. It has the structure of a question and the tonality or syntax of a statement or command.

"Your perception of school is changing, *isn't it.*" "You will do your home-work tonight, *won't you!*" Notice there is no question mark at the end of these sentences.

Communicating through a story or figure of speech

A metaphor is an indirect way of communicating through a figure of speech or story. It may, through the words used by the speaker, reveal the culture of his family or his deeper thoughts. It can also provide you with an effective way to communicate with another person at an unconscious level by offering solutions or suggestions (perhaps in the form of a fairy tale) or to quickly make a point. Recently, a friend and business colleague was modifying a highly successful course to satisfy a potential client. Essentially he was diluting the content. I made my point to him very clearly by saying, "A fine wine is no longer a fine wine when diluted." Metaphors are part of everyone's life, from the bedtime story, through the parables in the Bible, to the way you think of yourself and the way you dress.

Inner thoughts revealed

The deep structure of thought, based on feelings, memories, beliefs and values, is revealed through your behaviors. In individuals, this deep structure is referred to as your personality; in families, it might be referred to as family culture or "how we do things in this family."

At home, you may hear yourself or partner say, in a joking manner, "It's time to feed the animals." or "This place is a zoo." And often, it's not a joke. It's how this person perceives the activities within the family. Or you may have heard family members say, "It's time to do battle with the kids," or "bring out the big artillery" or "we need to outflank them." These are figures of speech analogous to wartime, and reveal the deep beliefs of an individual or a family – that life in the family is viewed as a battle. The metaphors you have for life, work or your family will, in turn, color how you see things. They will surface in your behaviors and in the words you use, and will influence your interactions with others.

Understanding a family's or family member's metaphor can provide insights to their inner feelings, memories, beliefs and values, and can provide you with an opportunity to be of assistance.

Consider the following example of two parents. One sees himself as a disciplinarian – a person who maintains order within the family – and the other views herself as a servant to the family's needs. Undoubtedly you would see distinct differences in their behaviors, including the words they use. Yet if we are *not* provided with this initial knowledge of how each parent views him- or herself, would it not still be possible to observe significant differences in their behaviors and to guess the metaphor that each carries?

People's behaviors give us insights into the metaphors they're living – if we're paying attention. Your metaphor may function at the spiritual level (purpose in life), as your identity or as a belief or value that you deem important. No matter which it is, it will have a distinct influence on your strategies and hence the behaviors you manifest.

Working with metaphors
If a person or family finds that their metaphors are not serving them, those metaphors can be changed to trigger different ways of thinking or to see the issue from a different perspective. You may assist your family or family member in changing their war metaphor – indicating conflict – to a sports metaphor – indicating competition. You can suggest new metaphors such as "move the ball forward," "avoid being offside," "need a big play." Or you may wish to take a non-competitive, win-win perspective and choose metaphors that help each family member see how they can support the others. Changing metaphors often gives you new insights and opportunities to pursue and can be a useful way to transfer learning or concepts between different contexts.

To determine a child's metaphor, listen to the words he uses and observe his behaviors. Alternatively, have him draw a picture of how he sees himself in the world, at school or at home. You can also ask him to draw a picture of how he would like to be in the future. This can be a very instructive exercise for the parent as well as the child, after which you can work on bridging the two metaphors.

Metaphors can be used in situations where you would like your listener to detach from their current situation and consider other possibilities. This is especially so in supporting your children – wherever there is potential for resistance, opposition or conflict. Metaphors provide you with helpful and useful communication and negotiation tools. It is difficult to argue with a good metaphor.

Metaphors communicate indirectly. An interesting story bypasses any conscious blocks or resistance and slips into the unconscious mind, where it triggers an unconscious search for meaning, resources and learnings appropriate for the listener. This is why fairy tales can have such a great impact on young children – especially those operating at the theta or alpha brainwave levels. Metaphors can be developed for a general audience (e.g., family), or for a specific person.

Creating a metaphor

To be successful, a metaphor must be engaging and reflect something of interest from the person's current experience or interest. Young children love stories and the more wondrous and magical, the better. With children, you are limited only by your imagination. So stretch yourself, have fun and make a real connection with your child by being an imaginative storyteller of stories that are engaging and have valuable lessons.

Many adults have (temporarily) lost the ability to tell good stories. During our NLP practitioner trainings, we help our adult learners reconnect with their storytelling abilities by asking them to construct a metaphor, giving them only five to ten minutes to do so. To further challenge them, we give them two or three words that must appear in the story. At a recent training, students were asked to write a metaphor that included the words "elephant" and "peanut." Here is the story written by Michelle Groleau and included with her permission.

Filomena and the Magic Peanut

"Mother," said Filomena, "if only I had a peanut to eat, everything would be wonderful. I'd be bigger, stronger and very powerful!"

"Filomena," her mother replied softly, "you're an elephant. You're already the biggest and the strongest animal in the jungle."

"But mother," argued Filomena, "elephants are supposed to eat peanuts. I've never even seen one. Surely, if I had one, I'd be even better, bigger and stronger than I am now." She walked away, head hanging low and dragging her trunk.

Filomena's mother thought for a while and decided to take a long walk to visit Kokoloco Bird, who was very well traveled. When she reached his home she called out, "Kokoloco Bird, may I have a moment of your time?"

The bird answered, "Of course, Mother Elephant, how may I help you?" Kokoloco Bird had impeccable manners.

"I was wondering . . . in your long journeys, have you possibly come across a peanut?" asked Mother. "It's for Filomena."

"No ma'am, I'm very sorry," replied Kokoloco Bird. "I have never seen a peanut, but I do have a vanilla bean that I would be very happy to give to you." Kokoloco Bird was very generous.

Mother accepted the vanilla bean, thanked Kokoloco Bird very much for his kindness and returned home with the vanilla bean in her trunk. She reached home just before sunset. Filomena ran out to greet her.

"Where were you, Mother?" said the girl elephant. "I was so worried!"

Mother only smiled and offered the vanilla bean to Filomena, who was so overjoyed that, without looking to see what it was, she took the bean into her trunk and quickly popped it into her mouth. She rolled it around on her tongue to savor it, then promptly swallowed it. A look of complete joy filled her face. She held her head high and stood tall. She shook her head so that her great ears flew back against her shoulders. Knowing she was going to grow bigger and stronger, she felt happier than she'd ever been before.

When Mother told her that what she had thought was a peanut was actually only a vanilla bean, Filomena looked confused. Suddenly she grinned widely as she realized that the magic to make her big and strong and powerful wasn't in a peanut after all. It was in her!

4.6 CHANGING A FEW WORDS CAN MAKE A DIFFERENCE

Sometimes changing just a few words can make a difference in what you or your children see as possible to achieve in life. It may be the words you say to yourself or to your children.

For example, when you get into a taxi and the driver asks you where you want to go, do you say:

- "I don't want to be here."
- "Try to take me to this address."
- "I should go to this address."

You probably don't say any of these things. I'm sure you are much clearer and more confident about where you want the taxi to take you. Then how is it that you are not as clear about what you want to achieve in your life?

Use care with negatives

Your unconscious mind cannot directly process a negative. Your unconscious mind first brings up the thought without the negation and then "puts a line through it." If I ask you to not think of a pink elephant, what do you think of? A pink elephant!

Your children arrive home from school. You say to them, "Don't eat the cookies." Your children had not even thought of cookies until you said this. Now you have a ten-minute discussion with your children about eating cookies. How often do you tell your children what not to do – "Don't play near the road" – instead of telling them what you would like them to do – "Play in the backyard"?

Notice how often you tell yourself what you don't want. By expressing what you don't want, you raise awareness of exactly the thing in question and significantly increase the chances of it happening. Remember the Law of Attraction – what you focus on is what you get!

What is your usual response to the question "How are you?" If you tend to reply with "Not bad," the next time you're asked this question, consider saying, *"Great!"* with matching voice tonality and physiology. Notice the effect this new response has on you as well as on the person who asked the question.

The use of negatives has its place and in some situations can be used to your advantage. Consider the following:

You are about to ask your child to undertake a very difficult task. You could say either "This task will be difficult" or "I *can't* say this task will be easy." Notice the different internal representations that each statement generates. Which do you think will be more appealing to your child? (That is, unless your child is a mismatcher. See sameness – difference meta program).

Use care with the word *try*

How often do you hear or say, "I'll try"? And what does this mean? Sometimes the word *try* is used to mean "I really don't want to do what you have asked, but I don't know how to say no to you" or "I don't have sufficient confidence in myself to make a full commitment to getting this done" or "I don't know what I really want in life."

When I hear people express their dreams or outcomes with the word *try*, I usually ask myself, "How serious is this person about achieving his dreams?" What messages is he sending to his unconscious mind? I see this as having one foot on the playing field and the other foot in the stands and hoping to score a touchdown. Highly unlikely! Trying is a waste of energy.

> *Try?* There is no *try*. There is only *do* or *not do*.
> – *Yoda, Star Wars: The Empire Strikes Back*

Should is another word similar to *try*. Are you one of those people who has a list of things they "should" do, yet rarely accomplishes any of the items on your list? Think back five years and notice how your life – career, relationships (with your children, parents or partner), health – would be different today, if you had actually accomplished some of the items on that *should* list, rather than letting them wither and fall away. Recall all the great *shoulds* you thought of doing for or with your children, great ideas that would have made a significant difference to your children, yet they never got to experience them with you. Or what about the *shoulds* you thought about with regard to your parents, and now you don't have the opportunity to carry them out? Or think of your current *should* list. How will your life be different later today, next week, next year or five years from now if you were to identify a few critical items on your *should* list and actually do them?

How would your life change, if instead of saying, "I will try to . . ." or "I should . . ." you say "I will get that done . . ." or "I am in the process of . . . ," while specifying a time when it will be done and focusing your actions on doing so?

Move from can't to possibility

Can't is a word used far too often and shuts out the possibility of doing and achieving something. If your child says, "I can't do math," this closes down any possibility of her being able to succeed at math. If instead you coach her to say, "I haven't yet found a way to do math," this leaves the door open to finding a solution and puts her, with your assistance, on a path of discovery.

Instead of you or your child saying what she can't do, what would happen and how would she feel if she talked about what she can do? "I can add, subtract, multiply and divide, and I haven't yet found a way to do algebra." This small change can have a significant effect on her attitude and how she feels about the task and her creativity.

And is often better than *but*

You have just finished sharing an idea with your child and the first word out of her mouth is "but . . ." What's your reaction? Do you think she was actually listening? Do you feel she has rejected your idea without even giving it any thought? Now assume she said "and" instead of "but." Does this feel different? Do you have the feeling she was listening and is now building on your idea?

The word *but* has the potential to diminish or kill whatever idea, thought or experience immediately precedes it. "You did very well on your homework, but you have a few errors that need correcting." Far too often we use *but* when *and* is a better choice. Begin to notice where in your conversation you can enhance your communication by using *and* in place of *but*.

There are definitely times when *but* is useful. Here are two situations where you can use *but* to your advantage.

- You want or feel you have to declare something, and then would like it to diminish or even disappear from the awareness of those who are listening. "As a family we haven't communicated as well as we could have, but that's in the past and we can do things differently now."
- You can use *but* as a pre-emptive move with someone who tends to respond with a "Yes, but." For example, let's say you want to present a suggestion to your partner, who you know from experience tends to find objections or respond negatively to other people's ideas. You can say, "You may think what I suggest won't work, but I'd like you fully consider it and let me know what you think." If your partner is someone who tends to take the opposite view (mismatcher), he will feel compelled to disagree with the idea before the *but*, particularly if you have a slight pause before proceeding with the *but* and the rest of your thought. This will tend to move him toward agreement with the second part of your sentence and be more likely to consider your suggestion on its merits.

Give a reason and get more compliance

Providing a reason for your request can increase your chances of having it acted on.

E. Langer, A. Blank and B. Chanowitz ("The Mindlessness of Ostensibly Thoughtful Action: The Role of 'Placebic' Information in Interpersonal Interaction," *Journal of Personality and Social Psychology*, 1978, Vol. 36, No. 6, 635–642) discovered if a reason was presented to a person when making a request, the person was more likely to comply than if no reason was presented, even if the reason conveyed no useful information.

The next time you want your child to do something, include a reason when you make your request. "Please tidy your room, because I feel happier when the house looks nice."

4.7 OVERVIEW OF THIS CHAPTER

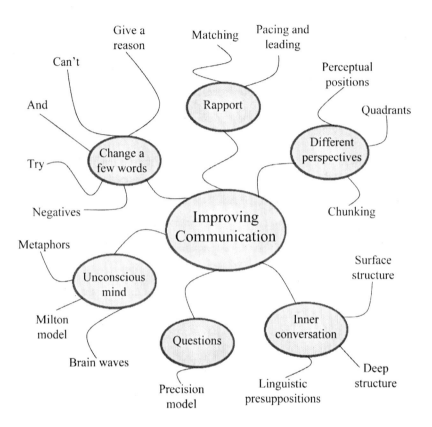

FIGURE 6: MIND MAP OF THIS CHAPTER:
IMPROVING YOUR COMMUNICATION

5.

Your Toolkit for Change

This chapter contains a number of NLP techniques, most of which the average reader will be able to effectively use for themselves or to assist other family members. Those trained at the NLP practitioner level or higher will find these techniques are already part of their toolkit or a valuable addition.

5.1 CHANGING YOUR PERCEPTION CHANGES YOUR REACTION

You use language of the mind – pictures, sounds, feelings, tastes, smells and words – to remember and make sense of a particular experience or to forecast a future experience. As we have discussed, these pictures, sounds, etc. are known as representational systems or modalities. Some of the pictures you make in your mind may be big, bright and in color, while others may be small, dark and black and white. These finer distinctions are called visual submodalities and define how you interpret, give meaning to or react to your internal representations – happy, excited, fearful, sad or just okay. In a similar manner there are finer distinctions (submodalities) for the other modalities. Sounds may be loud or soft, or coming from a particular direction. Feelings may be in different parts of the body or have different temperatures. Smells may be pleasant or offensive, strong or light. Taste may be sweet or bitter, strong or mild.

Generally, in NLP only three modalities (and corresponding submodalities) – visual, auditory and kinesthetic – are used. However, in certain situations – for example, those dealing with food – olfactory or gustatory submodalities may play a major role.

Some of the more common submodalities are:

EXAMPLE SUBMODALITIES		
Visual	**Auditory**	**Kinesthetic**
Black & white or color	Loud or soft	Strong or weak
Near or far	Near or far	Large or small area
Bright or dim	Internal or external	Weight: heavy or light
Location[4]	Location	Location in body
Size of picture	Stereo or mono	Constant or intermittent
Associated/dissociated[5]	Fast or slow	Temperature: hot or cold
Focused or defocused	High or low pitch	Size
Framed or unbounded	Rhythm	Shape
Moving or still	Clarity	Vibration
Flat or 3D	Pauses	Breathing rate

Key building block of NLP techniques

The submodalities you use to store your memories give meaning to those memories. You cannot change an event that has already happened; however, by adjusting the submodalities of the memory, you can change how you perceive it and respond to it. This is also true when you imagine future events. How you perceive the world around you defines your reality and establishes the base for what you

---

4. The location submodality refers to where the internal representation is located in your mind's eye. For the visual modality, the mental picture could be directly in front, to the left, up and to the right, and so on. For sound, it could be located in front of you, behind you or it might surround you. For a feeling, it could be in a particular part of the body or throughout your body.

5. The submodality Associated/Dissociated is very important. If you are associated in a memory, you are right in the action, viewing it from first position, or as we often say, "looking through your own eyes." In an associated state, your feelings (happy, sad, fearful) about that memory will be more intense. Being dissociated is more like watching a movie of your life (where you can see yourself in the movie rather than being involved) – any feelings will be less intense or nonexistent. If your child is addressing an issue that is very emotional or traumatic, it's advantageous to have him view his memory from a dissociated perspective.

achieve. A recent client had difficulty with his mother. When he thought of her, the image in his mind was big and very close – "in his face". By making this picture in his mind smaller and moving it farther away, he could "see" her differently and it opened the opportunity for a different relationship with her.

Submodalities are key components of many of the NLP techniques. Submodalities, by themselves or as part of other techniques, have been used to assist people to stop smoking, eat more of certain foods and less of others, change beliefs and values, enhance motivation, move from stress to relaxation, address phobias, and many other personal issues.

Being resourceful

Do you or your children find yourselves unresourceful – irritated, anxious, intimidated – when in the presence of a certain person? The following is an exercise that will assist you with changing how you feel and thus making better choices in your behaviors.

1. Think of someone with whom, when in their presence, you go into an unresourceful state. Close your eyes and form a picture of this person in your mind.[6] See what she looks like, hear how she sounds and notice how you feel.

2. Take this picture and make it black and white, shrink it down to a small picture and push it far away in your mind. If you like, you can make the picture look funny by putting a halo over her head or painting her hair blue.

3. Now change her voice. Make it sound softer, less demanding, ridiculous like Donald Duck's voice or squeaky like an old door opening.

4. Notice that you now feel differently.

5. Break state and repeat steps two to four several more times.

6. Now think of this person. Notice you now feel differently about her and feel more resourceful.

Adults and teenagers may be held back from achieving their dreams by having a picture or voice of a parent flash into their mind when they attempt to do something different or step outside of their limiting beliefs. The above exercise handles this situation very well.

---

6. For some of us, the pictures we make in our minds are very clear. For others, the picture is not clear; there is only a general sense of it being there, nevertheless if we're asked questions about its finer qualities (submodalities) we're able to answer accurately.

As a coach in the previous or similar exercises, rapport is important. Make it a fun experience – which may mean stepping out of your shell.

Changing behaviors

Sometimes the behaviors you manifest are less than you are capable of and in other situations you perform to your full potential. In the exercise below, using submodalities, you can shift how you perceive the first situation and make different choices in your behaviors – getting a more acceptable result.

1. On a piece of paper, construct a table with three columns. In the first column, list the names for the visual, auditory and kinesthetic submodalities. In column two, record the submodalities for the unwanted behavior (step two). In column three, record the submodalities for the desired behavior (step three).

2. Close your eyes and think of a situation in which you exhibited the undesired behavior. Elicit the submodalities (visual, auditory and kinesthetic) for this memory. When finished, break state (clears your mind of previous thoughts) by stretching, taking a deep breath or briefly looking around the room you're in.

    This should be done quickly. For example, once you have a picture, decide if it is black and white or color. Is it near or far? When you finish with the visual submodalities, do the same for the auditory and kinesthetic submodalities.

3. Close your eyes and think of a situation in which you exhibited the desired behavior. Elicit the submodalities for this memory. Then break state.

4. Compare column two with column three to determine which submodalities are different – these are called the critical submodalities.

    This process is called *contrastive analysis*. In column one, place an asterisk next to those submodalities that are different in columns two and three, as these are the only submodalities you will need to change in step five.

5. Close your eyes and recall the internal representation for the undesired behavior. Keep the content of the internal representation constant as you change the critical submodalities, one at a time, to those of the desired behavior.[7] This is called *mapping across*.

---

7. To illustrate, assume the content of your visual internal representation for the undesired behavior is a picture of you speaking uncomfortably to your teacher and that the submodalities are small and dark. Assume the desired behavior is a picture of you speaking powerfully with confidence to your friends and that the submodalities are large and bright. To map across, see the picture of you speaking to your teacher, while changing the small, dark picture to a large, bright picture.

6. Break state and test by going out into the future, where a similar situation may arise, and noticing how you feel or react given your new "view" of the situation (future pacing).

Putting issues in perspective

As you think about a current problem or issue, what are you focusing on? If the issue involves another person, in your mind you may well have a big, bright, close-up (in your face) picture of her. And if you were to replay her voice in your mind, you may hear it loud and clear with a specific tone that results in you feeling angry, dismissed or violated. All of this is in the foreground of your thoughts/mental images. Other information, including resources, are present in the background that you are currently choosing not to see, hear or feel as clearly or at all. What do you think would happen if you put less focus on what is in the foreground and more focus on what is in the background? Perhaps the problem or issue would not seem so big or the person so overbearing, and as a result you would be more resourceful.

The foreground – background technique is a simple process that assists you in becoming aware of what is in the background. You can then choose to give it more or all of your attention and hence be more resourceful or more conscious of other choices. It can be used in a variety of situations – to be more resourceful and comfortable when addressing a perceived problem, in the presence of authority figures, when receiving criticism, when in a situation that may generate anxiety, when feeling lost or disoriented or when responding to a need to eat, smoke or gamble in excess. As with any change technique, you must be prepared to respond differently. If there is secondary gain or if you harbor beliefs that restrict you in some way, these need to be addressed first.

1. Think of a current issue in which you would like to be more resourceful and have more choice in how you respond. Notice what you see in the foreground as you think of this issue. Also notice what sounds and feelings are in the foreground – those you are paying attention to. Now look, hear and feel beyond the foreground and become aware of what you have not been paying attention to in the background. Is there other useful information here?

2. Start with your focus on the images in the foreground, as has been the case up until now. As you do, make these images smaller, duller and less clear; at the same time, quickly bring the background forward to be big, bright and focused. Notice what you now see that you had not clearly seen before. You may even be more aware of what's going on all around you.

3. Enjoy this new awareness and notice what else is possible. Perhaps the issue is not as important or does not affect you as much as it did before. Break state.

4. Repeat steps two and three at least three times. Speed is important when interchanging the foreground and background.

5. Up to now, you have worked only with the visual modality. Here you will include any sounds. Notice what sounds are in the foreground and if they support you or not. If the sounds do not support you, have these sounds become less audible or less harsh, and allow supportive sounds or simply quiet from the background rush forward to replace them.

6. Enjoy this new awareness and notice what else is possible. Break state.

7. Repeat steps five and six at least three times.

8. Notice what feelings are in the foreground and if they support you or not. If the feelings don't support you, have these feelings become less intense or disappear altogether as other supportive, resourceful feelings (e.g., confidence, playfulness) or simply a sense of calmness or control rush forward to replace them.

9. Enjoy this new awareness and notice what else is possible and how you can choose to respond differently in the future. Break state.

10. Repeat steps eight and nine at least three times.

By focusing on the foreground, you make the problem or issue seem larger, preventing you from seeing it in the full context. By making the foreground smaller and putting more attention on the background, you put the issue in perspective and can see, hear or feel it as something you can overcome.

5.2 MAKING THE MOST OF YOUR AUTOMATIC RESPONSES

We all have automatic responses to certain stimuli. For example, if you're driving down the road and you see a red light, instinctively your foot moves to the brake. Or perhaps you arrive home a little tired and in the air is the smell of your favorite food and you immediately perk up. Or you think of someone you don't enjoy being with and immediately feel angry or irritated.

The Nobel Prize-winning scientist and physiologist Ivan Pavlov identified the notion of stimulus response. He observed that if he gave food to his dogs and simultaneously rang a bell, the dogs came to associate the sound of the bell with food and would salivate when they heard the bell, even if no food was present. Here, the stimulus is the bell and the response is salivating.

In NLP, we refer to stimulus response as *anchoring*. The stimulus (the anchor or trigger) may come from your external environment – perhaps this is a certain touch, seeing a red traffic light or a favorite cup or shirt. Alternatively, it may be an internal representation – seeing in your mind your children's faces, for example. In any case, it triggers a conscious or unconscious internal response or feeling that may result in a behavioral response.

The following are examples of anchors. Can you add to this list?

- Seeing your country's flag raised at the Olympics – external visual.
- Police siren – external auditory.
- Wearing your favorite team's jersey – external visual/kinesthetic.
- A gentle touch by a loved one – external kinesthetic.
- The taste of a favorite food – external gustatory.
- A teacher says the word *test* – external auditory digital (a word).
- An image of your child in your mind – internal visual.
- Your mother says your full name or your childhood nickname in a certain tone of voice – external auditory/auditory digital.

Anchors can be very useful, and they can also be counterproductive. Most anchors operate outside of your conscious awareness and have an impact on your mental state or behavior despite the fact that you may be unaware of them. Useful anchors are those that generate pleasant memories or put you into a motivated, confident or empowered state, or those that result in a useful behavior – a red light is ahead; you slow and stop the car. Examples of counterproductive anchors are:

- You are a fully functioning adult until you step across the threshold of your parent's house, when you may take on certain less than resourceful behaviors.
- Your child panics when her teacher says there will be a quiz in five minutes.
- You got sick eating a certain food. Now whenever you think of that food you feel sick.
- Your child makes a comment, using a certain tone of voice and body language, and you react in a less than resourceful manner.
- Someone touches you unexpectedly, and this brings up past memories of an unpleasant event.

Influencing the response you trigger in other people
Certain venues serve as anchors. Some relate to pleasant experiences, others to less than pleasant experiences. In the latter case, these venues can be disempowering because they arouse certain emotions and thus threaten relaxed and open dialogue. If you want to speak with your children or have a family meeting where everyone can feel safe and speak freely as equals, be aware that certain rooms may be anchors for members of your family – a room where family

disagreements often occur, or Dad's office or workshop. You may wish to meet at a neutral or positive site located outside of the house. Or establish a room in the house that is anchored only with positive energy – that is, any heated discussions are handled elsewhere.

The manner, in which you address other people – your tone of voice, the words you choose and your body language – has the potential to establish an anchor in other people, especially if this behavior is repeated several times. If you use the same room of your house, and you have a specific body language and tone of voice every time you discipline your children, you will set up an anchor to one or more of these triggers. You may wonder why they seem reserved every time you invite them into that room and you take a similar body language and tone of voice. It's quite simple; you are firing off negative anchors.

In a similar manner, you can establish positive anchors that at an unconscious level will have them feel good about being with you.

Understanding and using anchors enables you to:

• Access positive feelings and resource states, such as confident or loved.
• Transfer an anchor.
• Override undesired feelings and thoughts.

Basic anchoring concepts

You can change those anchors that do not generate the results you want or create new anchors to put you in a resourceful state or react in a desired fashion. Anchors can be created by chance or intentionally in two ways:

1. In a single occurrence, if it happens during a highly emotional, positive or negative event. For example, your partner may have taken you to a special place and proposed to you in a very romantic and emotional way. When you return to this location, what comes to mind?

2. Through repetition and the continual association between a stimulus and a response. Repetition is needed if the emotion is weak or there is no emotional involvement at all. Television commercials often link an alcoholic beverage with a pleasant experience. After seeing this advertisement a number of times, you begin to make the pleasant association.

An intentionally created anchor (trigger), which can be visual, auditory, kinesthetic or auditory digital, should be:

• Unique, distinct and easy to repeat. It should not have other previous associations. If touching your thumb and index finger together is not something you do routinely, this would be an effective kinesthetic anchor. Saying a word internally in a particular tone of voice would be a good auditory digital and auditory anchor. Selecting a trigger that you inadvertently fire often has the potential of dissipating quickly – rendering it useless. Unique anchors or triggers are best and longer-lasting.

- Linked to a resource state that is cleanly and completely re-experienced. Your child may wish to create an anchor enabling him to feel confident in certain situations. However, if he is confused about your instructions for setting the anchor, the resulting anchor may generate a response that is a mixture of confidence and confusion.

- Timed just as the state is reaching its peak. For example, when assisting your child, as he recalls a time when he possessed a certain attribute (e.g., confidence), his feeling of confidence will begin to get stronger until it reaches a peak. Have him use his sensory acuity (you can assist by using your sensory acuity as well) and apply the anchor (trigger) when he notices he is beginning to access this state and hold the trigger until the state peaks. Depending on how fast your child accesses his feelings, the anchor can be applied anywhere from several seconds to ten seconds. Applying the anchor past the peak may result in picking up a weakened or other unwanted state.

The basic steps for creating an anchor for you or your children are:

1. Recall a past vivid experience for the state to be anchored.

2. Apply a specific anchor as the state is reaching its peak.

3. Break state.

4. Test by setting off (firing) the anchor. Is the state accessed?

5. Repeat steps one through three several times to make the anchor stronger. This is called *stacking* an anchor.

The best state to anchor is a naturally occurring state (e.g., laughing at a joke you just heard). The next best state is a past, vivid, highly associated state. To create an anchor for a specific state you have never experienced, think of someone who possesses that quality – this person can be real or imaginary. Imagine stepping into that person's shoes and taking on her physiology and feelings when she is in that state.

To elicit a past memory for anchoring purposes, use the following script:

Remember a specific time when you were really _____ (e.g., confident). Close your eyes and fully associate into that memory by going back to that time, putting yourself in your own body, looking through your own eyes, seeing what you saw, hearing what you heard and having the feelings of being really _____.

When helping your child access a particular state, you can assist her by using a voice tonality that reflects the state she is accessing. If this is an energetic state, your voice tonality should reflect energy.

To maintain an anchor, only fire it when necessary, and regularly reinforce it. To reinforce or build up an anchor: 1) regularly repeat the process used to establish the anchor, or 2) if you are naturally experiencing the desired state, fire the trigger to enhance the anchor.

To enhance the strength of the anchor or to associate different resources to the same anchor, you can stack the anchors; that is, repeat the anchoring process several times by eliciting several occurrences of the same or different states, and anchor them with the same trigger.

Accessing positive feelings and states

Would it be useful to call up a specific resource – such as confidence – whenever you felt your confidence waning? Or perhaps your child would like to have a variety of resources at her command (confidence, energy, excitement, humor) when she speaks in front of her class. This calls for a *resource* anchor. The steps for creating a resource anchor for yourself are as follows. Modify accordingly, if assisting your children with establishing a resource anchor.

1. Identify the situation in which you would like to be more resourceful.

2. Identify the resource(s) that you would like to have available.

3. Establish what the anchor – the trigger or stimulus – will be.

    The anchor should be easy to fire, inconspicuous and only fired when you choose. I prefer to use a kinesthetic anchor. Suggestions are: touching your right ear with your right hand, touching your index finger and thumb together or making a fist in a different fashion than you ordinarily do.

4. Think of a time when you experienced that resource and elicit the state. Use the elicitation script mentioned above.

5. When you feel the state achieving about two-thirds of its peak, fire the anchor and hold it until the state peaks, then release.

6. Repeat steps four and five at least five times to establish and stack the anchor.

7. Test the association by firing the anchor and confirming that you are experiencing the desired state. If not, or if the state is not strong enough, repeat steps four and five.

The following are some variations on the above:

- You may wish to have several different resources associated with a specific anchor. For example, in addition to confidence, you may also wish to be energetic and excited. In this case, repeat steps four and five and introduce a different resource with the same trigger.
- To make the elicited state stronger in step four, you may wish to adjust the submodalities or take on a physiology that reflects the desired state.

Remember, you cannot change other people. However, by being more resourceful, you can choose to adopt different behaviors when dealing with them. For others to continue communicating with you, they will have to modify their behaviors or withdraw from the communication.

Transferring a resource anchor

It's common for young children to have an external resource anchor – teddy bear, old blanket. These are perfect resource anchors as they help your child generate feelings of safety, comfort, confidence and love. When it's time for him to go to school or other public venue, however, it may not be appropriate for him to bring his favorite blanket with him. In this situation, you can transfer the anchor to something more appropriate – a wristband or pendant. Have fun doing this and really use your imagination.

You may decide to transfer the anchor to a special stone. Start by making it an adventure to find this stone. If he has fun finding this special stone, those good feelings will already be anchored to it. Once he finds the stone, you can hold it in a special way and let him know that you are transferring your love for him to the stone, so whenever he needs your support, all he needs to do is touch the stone. Now have him hold his blanket and absorb all the good feelings from the blanket. As these feelings begin to build, have him pick up the stone and imagine all these good feelings being shared between the blanket and the stone. Reinforce what he has done by letting him know that he now has a choice of using his blanket or his special stone and that both will work for him.

Overriding undesired feelings and thoughts

Sometimes, when an anchor fires, you may find yourself in a problem state when you really want to react in a more positive way. Perhaps when your partner or parents make a comment in a certain tone of voice, you react by becoming angry, sulking or withdrawing. Or you may feel dismissed or stupid, when looked at in a certain way. *Collapsing* anchors is a technique that can resolve problems such as these.

The process of collapsing anchors is based on the notion that if one anchor is much stronger than another, and both are fired at the same time, the stronger anchor will overwhelm the weaker one. This technique uses a kinesthetic anchor;

therefore, you should have permission to touch an appropriate spot – say, the knuckles – of the person you are assisting before proceeding. If you don't do this, you may surprise her and she may not feel safe – instead, she'll wonder how or where you may touch her next. Although this process can also be done with a visual or auditory anchor, I find that a kinesthetic anchor works best. The following process is written for a parent assisting his child.

1. Assist your child with identifying the problem state or experience.

2. Have your child close her eyes and recall the problem state or experience, fully associated, looking through her own eyes, seeing what she saw, hearing what she heard and feeling what she felt at the time. Anchor by touching a specific knuckle.

3. Break state.

4. Test the negative "problem" anchor by firing it, to ensure it is established. Your child should be feeling and taking on the physiology of the problem state.

5. Break state.

6. Have your child identify a positive resource state or several different resource states by asking her how she would like to react or feel instead.

7. Have your child recall the positive, resourceful state, fully associated, looking through her own eyes, seeing what she saw, hearing what she heard and feeling what she felt at the time. Anchor by touching a different knuckle.

8. Break state.

9. Repeat steps six to eight until you have built up a powerful positive anchor.

    You can stack the same positive state or stack a number of different states. The key is to ensure that this positive anchor is bigger and more powerful than the negative anchor. Use the same knuckle, even if you are using different positive resource states.

10. Have your child close her eyes while you fire both anchors at the same time.

    Carefully observe your child's physiology. You are looking for some shift – signs of change or confusion – to indicate that the integration is complete. This shift may be obvious: her head may jerk back, or her face may become flushed; or less obvious: her eyelids may flutter slightly or her hands twitch. Each person reacts differently.

11. Once you have observed this shift, release the negative anchor.

12. Hold the positive anchor for an additional five seconds, then release.

13. Test and future pace.

> To future pace, have your child imagine a future situation where, in the past, she would have reacted with the unresourceful state. What happens now as she thinks of this future event?

5.3 EXPANDING BEYOND SELF-IMPOSED LIMITS

A picture frame places borders or boundaries around what you can see in a picture. In a similar fashion, the frames of reference you choose as a result of your beliefs about yourself and others, your perceived role in life, and your perceived limitations in skills or abilities can limit what you see as possible; alternatively, they can open up all sorts of possibilities. You (and others, if you allow them) are continually setting time frames, psychological boundaries and physical limits on what you can or can't do – often without any real thought about the consequences or the reality of those limitations.

Changing the frame of an experience can have a major influence on how you perceive, interpret and react to that experience. Knowing you have one hour to complete a task will most likely result in a different emotional state, approach and quality of work than if you know you have one week to accomplish the same task. This illustrates how a change in frame – in this case a time frame – can have a significant impact on the choices you make. In NLP, changing the frame of reference is called *reframing*. The purpose of reframing is to help you expand beyond your current thoughts, beliefs, limitations and actions to become more resourceful and have more choice in finding solutions to your problems.

Reframing goes on all around you:
- Politicians are masters at reframing. It seems no matter what happens, they can create a positive spin for themselves or a negative spin for their opponents.
- Consider that old wooden table in the basement that you use as a temporary workbench for sawing wood and doing household repairs. What if someone were to tell you it is a valuable antique? Instantly, your old worktable is transformed into a thing of value.
- Jokes are reframes. You are guided to think in one frame and then the frame – the meaning or context – changes.
- All metaphors assist us in seeing things from a different perspective.
- Fairy tales often use reframes in the form of analogies or metaphors to help children see different perspectives or consequences.
- An excuse is a reframe that attributes a different meaning or context to your behaviors.

Here are some further notable examples of reframes:

- During the 1984 U.S. presidential campaign, there was considerable concern about Ronald Reagan's age. Speaking during the presidential debate with Walter Mondale, Reagan said, "I will not make age an issue of this campaign. I am not going to exploit, for political purposes, my opponent's youth and inexperience." Reagan's age was not an issue for the remainder of the campaign!
- There is a story about Thomas Watson, Sr., the first president of IBM. A young worker had made a mistake that lost IBM one million dollars in business. She was called in to the president's office for a discussion. As she walked in, she said, "Well, I guess you've called me here to fire me." "Fire you?" Mr. Watson replied. "I just spent a million dollars on your education!"
- A father brought his headstrong daughter to see Milton Erickson, the famous hypnotherapist. He said to Erickson, "My daughter doesn't listen to me or her mother. She is always expressing her own opinions." After the father finished describing his daughter's problem, Erickson replied, "Now isn't it good that she'll be able to stand on her own two feet when she is ready to leave home?" The father sat in stunned silence. That was the extent of the therapy – the father now saw his daughter's opinionated behavior as a useful resource later in her life.

Changing the meaning or the context

In NLP, there are two basic forms of reframes – *content* (or meaning) and *context* reframes.

Content reframe

What you choose to focus on or how you interpret an event determines the content or meaning you have chosen to assign to it. An electrical power failure may be viewed as a disruptive, major disaster, given all you have to accomplish. Alternatively, it may be viewed as an opportunity to spend some intimate time with your partner, or to have fun with your children finding innovative ways to manage the situation.

A content reframe is useful in situations where your child says something such as, "I hate it when my teacher stands behind me while I'm working on an assignment." Although you don't know the exact interpretation or meaning your child has assigned to her teacher's behavior, it's clear that her interpretation limits her resourcefulness and possible courses of action. To assist your child in moving to a more resourceful state, gain clarity on the meaning she has assigned to her teacher's behavior by asking questions such as, "How is his behavior a problem for you?" or "What meaning have you assigned to his behavior?" Her answer(s) may give you insights into different interpretations you can provide that she has not thought of. To assist you in identifying these other interpretations:

- Explore what other meaning her teacher's behavior could have. For example, an NLP presupposition states, "Every behavior has a positive intention." This may lead you to asking your child, "Is it possible he wants to help and doesn't know how to offer his assistance in any other way?"
- Look at the perceived benefits to your child. A possible reframe might be, "Isn't it great that you know your boundaries and you're not prepared to allow someone to violate them?"
- Identify opportunities this situation provides. "Since your teacher is right beside you, why not take the opportunity to get his help with the questions you don't understand?"

Context reframe
Almost all attributes or behaviors are useful or appropriate in some context. A context reframe is useful for statements such as, "I'm too young" or "I wish I didn't always focus on what might go wrong." In these situations, your child has assumed that being young or exhibiting this behavior has little or no value. Your role is to discover when it can be of value by asking yourself the questions, "When would this attribute be viewed as a resource?" Or "Where would this behavior be viewed as useful? A possible reframe for the former might be, "Think of the advantage you have over the others because you're younger – you have time to learn new skills and to be more successful than they are." And for the latter, "Isn't focusing on what might go wrong a great skill to have when you need to avoid potential problems?"

The first reframe changes the context of time, while the second changes the context to one of "avoiding potential problems." Other context changes you can explore are:

- Perceptual positions. Explore the situation from the different perceptual positions. Perhaps you're annoyed by your child's behavior, yet when explored from her perspective (second position) or from the context of the overall system (fourth position), it is most appropriate.
- Different locations. A behavior may be inappropriate at school and very acceptable at home or in the playground.

Additional points to consider
When presenting a reframe to another person:

- Make sure you have rapport and their permission to provide them with a different perspective (reframe).
- You may believe your reframe is the best ever and yet it may not work for the other person – simply because she has a different model of the world than you do. Remember the NLP presupposition that there is no failure, only feedback, and explore other possible reframes.

- If you present the reframe in the form of a question or a metaphor, it will most likely be considered more fully than if you present it as a statement of fact.
- Avoid getting caught up in your own limitations. To offer an effective reframe, you must step outside of the other person's model of the world, which may be constrained by many of the same limiting beliefs that you have.

Children and parenting

Children exhibit all sorts of behaviors – some appropriate and some not so appropriate. Focusing mainly on a child's inappropriate behaviors may result in him feeling overly criticized or attacked, which in turn may cause an increase in problem behavior or your child to become defiant or defensive. If your child has a behavior that you find inappropriate, the two of you can use the following process to identify a different behavior that is acceptable to both of you.

1. Identify the behavior you're having difficulty with. Acknowledge that in the right place or time, this can be a valued behavior, and this place or time is not appropriate.
2. Work with your child to identify the positive intention behind his behavior.
3. Assist him in generating as many alternative behaviors (which may involve a specific place or time or you doing something different) as possible that satisfy this positive intention. From this list, identify three alternative behaviors that you both support.
4. Allow him to select one from this list of three.

5.4 USING YOUR BODY FOR A CHANGE

When NLP was first developed, it was mainly focused on the conscious manipulation of internal representations; for example, adjusting submodalities. That is, the unconscious mind was often not directly engaged in the process. Realizing this, John Grinder and Judith DeLozier developed NLP new code, which involves your unconscious mind and often your body in effecting long-lasting change. The following two exercises, which are from NLP new code, involve using the body and are great exercises to use with children (and adults), as it gets them fully involved with you in a playful manner.

Walking with Grace and Power

Walking with grace and power is a kinesthetic exercise, does not require the participation of the conscious mind (other than to maintain a state of excellence), and makes use of the connection between your internal representations and your physiology. That is, maintaining a positive and resourceful physiology while thinking of a less than resourceful experience helps to "rewire" your neurology and overwrite the less than resourceful response. As with many NLP processes, it is not necessary for the "coach" to know the issue the other person is addressing.

Walking is just one way to use this exercise. If your child is capable of other kinesthetic activities that require a fair degree of concentration to maintain excellence – dancing, drumming, juggling, Tai-Chi, martial arts – these can be used as an alternative. When coaching your child, you must understand the activity well enough to spot slips from excellence and be able to suggest corrections. The excellence state must be maintained for several minutes before the non-resourceful situation is reintroduced in order to activate the full physiological biochemistry. If the physiology deteriorates, the non-resourceful situation is set aside until excellence is restored in the walking or other kinesthetic state. The basic steps are as follows:

1. Identify a situation where your child responds with an undesired behavior or in a less than optimal way, and he would like to behave in a more resourceful or appropriate manner. Now set the situation aside for the moment.

2. Have your child walk in a pattern that is a minimum of ten to twelve feet (e.g., a figure eight or back and forth). As he walks, coach him by suggesting changes to his physiology (altering the position of his head, neck, shoulders, breathing pattern, posture, length of stride, position of feet, etc.) so that he is walking with grace and power (elegance, confidence, authority).

3. Have your child continue walking, while you monitor that the new style is being maintained.

4. When your child has maintained the walk (with grace and power) for a couple of minutes, coach him to think his way through the situation identified in step one. Continue monitoring the quality of his walk. If the quality falters, encourage him to return to the resourceful state in step two.

5. Once your child can completely think through the issue in step one from beginning to end while maintaining the quality of his walk, stop.

6. Test and future pace.

Alphabet Game

The Alphabet Game is a kinesthetic new code exercise developed by John Grinder and Roger Tabb. The intention is to occupy the conscious mind with physical activity while the unconscious mind unhooks a non-resourceful state from an experience or situation. This is reinforced through *cross-lateral processing* – the use of both hemispheres of the brain in a whole-brain manner (simultaneous processing).

To begin, the first twenty-five letters of the alphabet are written (in capital letters) in five rows and five columns. Then, below each of the twenty-five letters, place one of the following three lowercase letters, *l* for left, *r* for right and *t* for together, with the following restrictions: start by placing *l* under R, *r* under L and *t* under T and ensure no more than two of the lowercase letters are in a row or column. For example (you can use this chart, if you like):

A	B	C	D	E
l	r	t	t	l
F	G	H	I	J
t	l	r	l	r
K	L	M	N	O
r	r	l	t	l
P	Q	R	S	T
r	t	l	l	t
U	V	W	X	Y
t	l	r	r	t

1. Make the letters big enough so you can easily read them. Place this chart on the wall at eye height. Stand a few feet away from the wall.

2. Identify an issue that is bothering you and associate into the problem – fully experience the situation.

3. Break state and go to another part of the room and from there, identify the resources you need to address this issue. Fully associate into having these resources – if the resources are confidence and energy, remember or imagine a situation where you had confidence. Now stand and move as if you have confidence. Continuing to be confident, remember or imagine a situation where you had energy. Now move back to the position in front of the chart, bringing these resources with you.

4. Play the game, as follows:

   a. Begin by holding your hands waist-high.

b. Call out the letter A, while raising your left arm out to your side, shoulder-high, then lower your arm.

c. Call out the letter B, while raising your right arm out to your side, shoulder-high, then lower your arm.

d. Call out the letter C while together raising both arms shoulder-high and jumping off the ground, then lower your arms.

e. Call out the letter D while together raising both arms shoulder-high and jumping off the ground, then lower your arms.

f. And so on until you have gone through the alphabet in a forward direction.

g. Repeat starting at the letter Y and working your way through the alphabet backward.

h. Repeat going up and down columns and/or back and forth across the rows in a serpentine fashion. In this way, you'll get a less familiar order of the letters, thereby increasing your concentration.

i. Steps b. through h. are to be done as fast as you can, taking into account your physical abilities.

5. During step four, your coach makes sure you are saying the correct letter and doing the corresponding movement, as fast as you can. The quality of your state while playing this game will determine the quality of the changes you will experience when you next experience the issue that is bothering you.

6. Once you have successfully completed step four, stand relaxed and experience (using all of your senses) a new state for the issue being considered. Make sure to note anything new you've learned about this situation.

Once you have become proficient at this game, you can make it more challenging extending the left arm and the right leg, or the right arm and the left leg, or raise both arms and legs while jumping. This will further add to the cross-lateral processing.

5.5 WORKING WITH STRATEGIES – HOW YOU DO WHAT YOU DO

A strategy is the means by which you organize your thoughts and behaviors to accomplish a specific outcome. A strategy is also known as a habit, process, plan, approach, procedure, pattern or program. Everything you do is based on a strategy, most of which are outside of your conscious awareness. You have strategies for being healthy, being depressed, being bored, problem solving, remembering/

forgetting, falling in love, parenting, playing, being angry, having fun, over-eating, to name just a few. Some strategies may play out over several weeks or months – for example, when buying a special gift; others, like becoming angry, may fire in the blink of an eye.

From the logical levels, remember that strategies reflect your beliefs and values and provide a context for your behaviors. A strategy always aims for a positive outcome – as viewed from the strategy owner's model of the world. From another person's perspective, the outcome may not be considered positive. However, the strategy owner feels it's the best choice available given his view of the world and the resources he believes he has available. Most strategies run at an unconscious level and you really don't have to think about what to do. You just go through the motions and – *voila* – the result is achieved.

Strategies can be useful
Some strategies are useful. If every day you had to rediscover how to shower, shave, dress, make breakfast, and look after the children, life would be too busy and exhausting to get anything else done. Consider, for example, the following strategy:

Suppose it's a school day and it's time to get the children up and ready for school. Everyone has a designated role – even if it is simply to stay out of the way and let others do what is necessary. Notice there is a particular order in how things are done – who gets up first, how breakfast is prepared, when showers are taken, use of the bathroom, etc. When this particular order is followed, everything runs smoothly. If things get out of order, confusion and chaos are possible. Without having this overall strategy for getting the children ready for school, you would have to reinvent it every morning. Thus, things would be confusing and possibly not everything would get done.

Strategies can limit what's possible

> However beautiful the strategy, you should
> occasionally look at the results.
> – *Winston Churchill*

Strategies may create an illusion of safety and comfort, locking you into known paths and processes. Young children are not locked into these paths of habit, safety and comfort, which is why they're more creative than adults and their thinking is not as restricted. However, conditioning at home and school soon locks them into "the correct way" of doing something and their creativity becomes limited. For example:

If you want to enter or leave a room, you have a general approach (strategy) to do this. Within this strategy, you have learned that if the door is closed and it has a doorknob, by reaching out and twisting this doorknob you can open the door unless it's locked. Let's call this the *doorknob strategy*.

In an interesting experiment, a group of researchers moved the doorknob from its usual location to the other side of the door where the hinge was, and twisting the doorknob or pushing or pulling on it would not open the door. They then populated the room with adults. After a while, the adults decided they wanted to leave and so used their doorknob strategy. They pushed and pulled and twisted the knob; however, the door would not open. Hence, in their real-ity, they concluded the door was locked and they were locked in the room. In a subsequent part of the experiment, the researchers put young children into the same room. These children were not old enough to have fully developed the "doorknob" strategy, so they simply went up to the door, pushed on it until it opened, then left the room.

Here we had fully functioning adults who thought they were locked in a room when they were in fact not locked in. They (unconsciously) relied on a strategy that works most of the time, and they did not take into account the fact that there might be exceptions.

Here's a question for you. Where in your life, and with which family members, do you have a strategy for interacting with them that leaves you with the perception of being locked in, when in reality you are not locked in and have choices on how to act differently and achieve different results?

I'm sure you've heard people say, "Well, that's the way I've always done it." Perhaps it's time to become curious and explore whether your strategies are still meeting your needs. For me, one of the biggest benefits of NLP is to become consciously aware of what I am achieving. If I don't like the result, I can explore and change the strategy that generates it.

How are strategies created?
From infancy onward, our primary way of learning is trial and error. We do something and consciously or unconsciously assess the feedback. Have we been punished or rewarded for our actions? If we feel we've been punished, we alter our actions and do something different the next time. If we feel we've been rewarded, we internalize what we have done and run the program again and again – and a strategy is born. As we developed other strategies, they became organized together to compose our capabilities.

You have considerable influence on the current and future strategies of your children. Children model what the important people in their lives do. Whether you approach your parenting roles or interaction with those outside the family with self-confidence or apprehension, expect your children to do so as well. If you have a particular way of interacting with your partner or children, don't be surprised if your children do the same when they have a family.

Understanding the basic components of a strategy

A common analogy for describing a strategy is that of a recipe (e.g., baking a cake). The basic components are: criteria (how you know if you're on track or when you've finished), ingredients (representational systems), the appropriate quantities and qualities of the ingredients (submodalities) and a specific order or series of steps. If the ingredients or quantities and qualities are changed, it is not the same cake. If the order is changed – adding the eggs after the cake has been baked – you have something very different.

A strategy is a recipe and has four crucial aspects:

- Criteria that must be satisfied to achieve the end result.
- The sequence of the steps.
- The representational systems used.
- The distinctions within the representation systems – the submodalities.

In this book, only the first two are discussed.

Improving strategies for better results

Consider the following situation: Your child is getting As in history and Ds and Fs in mathematics. Obviously she has a good strategy for how to study history. Exploring her different approaches (strategies) for studying these two subjects may turn up useful differences.

The first things you can explore for each of these subjects are the criteria she uses to know if she is making progress and when she has achieved her desired result. Let's say you discuss this with her and find that, for history, her criteria are: useful, fun and gets her attention from others. For mathematics her criteria are: number of hours spent studying and gets her attention from others.

Examine how she approaches each subject. For history, she:

- Reviews the material in small chunks.
- Sees in her mind the various events and gets a feeling for what it would be like living at that time.
- Checks, at regular intervals, how this new information is linked to what she already knows and how it makes what she knows more useful. Discovering these linkages is fun.
- Can hardly wait to demonstrate to friends, family and teachers what she has learned.

For mathematics, she:

- Takes all of the material as one big chunk and simple bulls her way through it.
- Says the mathematical concepts to herself, hoping to remember a few formulae.
- Does not see how the material fits together and feels her time studying is a waste.
- Takes some consolation in being recognized as a hard worker.

Do you see any significant differences here? What do you think would happen if, for mathematics, you coached her to:

- Review the material in small chunks.
- See in her mind the various concepts and get a good feeling for how this information can be useful.
- Check, at regular intervals, how this material builds on what she already knows and how this new knowledge can be useful in managing her money or getting a better understanding how mathematics played a role in history – inventions, computing, material resources to support a war campaign, and so on.
- Get excited about demonstrating her new abilities to friends, family and teachers.

To install a strategy or habit, the key is to use the new strategy for five to thirty days. The more you encourage your child to use the new habit and not the old, the more the old habit begins to fade away. If she slips and uses the old habit during this period, simply coach her to realize that it is small step backward and she will have to focus on the new habit for a few more days.

A strategy for creativity

Walt Disney was known for his creativity and successful implementation of his ideas. When working on a new project, Disney used three distinct perspectives – dreamer, realist, and critic – and had rules on when and how the different perspectives interacted with each other. He would encourage his team to participate in these perspectives along with him and would create an environment that encouraged each perspective at the appropriate time. The following is based on the work of Robert Dilts (*Strategies of Genius*, Volumes I, II and II, 1994–5, Meta Publications), who developed a model for how Walt Disney was able to be creative and bring his ideas to life.

The Dreamer:
- Vision: The big picture, anything is possible.

The Realist:
- Action: Viewed from first position – fully associated. What does it feel like to be part of this dream? Act as if the dream is possible and develop a plan to realistically reach the dream.

The Critic:
- Logic: Viewed from second position (fully dissociated from any ownership of the dream). As a recipient or consumer of the final product, what is your reaction? What are the risks? Ensure quality and avoid problems by looking at the proposed plan under various "what if" scenarios.

Disney had a very clean and distinct separation between these perspectives. He insisted that each be completed before going to the next one. For each perspective, he used different locations and often included different people for the discussions.

The following is a powerful exercise to assist your children in planning their futures, to assist your family in determining a vision with action steps to attain it, or for you to expand your horizons on parenting or other important areas in your life. The basic steps are:

1. Select three different physical locations and label them Dreamer, Realist and Critic. If possible, you can even decorate the spaces accordingly.

2. Anchor the appropriate strategy to each physical location, and make sure you break state in between. For each strategy, use these techniques:

    a. Dreamer: Recall a time and take on the physiology of a dreamer – perhaps leaning back gazing at the sky – at a time when you were able to creatively dream up new ideas without any limitations. Anchor this to the first location.

    b. Realist: Recall a time and take on the physiology you had in a situation where you were able to think very realistically and were able to develop a plan to put your ideas into action. Anchor this to the second location.

    c. Critic: Recall a time and take on the physiology you had in a situation where you were able to identify key problems and provide constructive criticism. Anchor this to the third location.

3. Pick an outcome that you wish to achieve. Physically step into the Dreamer location and assume the appropriate physiology. See yourself accomplishing the outcome and think about it in a free and unrestricted manner. Identify the benefits. You may wish to answer the following questions:

- What do you want to achieve and for what purpose?
- What are the benefits and how will you know when you have achieved them?
- When will the benefits occur?
- What will this outcome lead to?
- Who will you be when you achieve this outcome?

Once this is complete, step out of this location and break state.

4. Step into the Realist location and assume the appropriate physiology. Associate fully into the dream and develop a course of action for achieving the dream (including time frames, milestones and resources). You may wish to answer the following questions:

- How will the outcome be achieved?
- How will you measure progress and know when you have achieved the outcome?
- What resources do you need, and what are the key outputs and time frames?
- Where will it be done?
- Are all the steps in the plan necessary? Are some missing?

Once this is complete, step out of this location and break state.

5. Step into the Critic location and assume the appropriate physiology. Identify potential problems and phrase criticisms as questions for the dreamer or realist – criticize the plan or the details of the dream, not the dream, the dreamer or the realist. Typical questions to address are:

- Who will be affected by this outcome? What are their needs, concerns and expectations? Why might they object?
- Are there benefits of the status quo? Should some be maintained?
- Will the plan assist you in achieving the outcome?
- Are there times and places that should be avoided?
- What could stop this outcome from being achieved?

Once this is complete, step out of this location and break state.

6. Step into the Dreamer location, assuming the appropriate physiology. Creatively develop solutions to the questions raised by the Critic.

7. Continue to revisit steps four, five and six until all three positions support your outcome and plan.

A strategy for family meetings

Edward de Bono's six hats (*Six Thinking Hats*, 2nd edition, Back Bay Books, 1999) provides a process for gaining clarity and developing a course of action to address an issue or explore a desired outcome. Although not part of the formal NLP body of knowledge, *Six Thinking Hats* illustrates the value of the NLP concept of viewing an issue from different perspectives, contexts or frames.

De Bono identified six different perspectives and referred to them as hats, each with their own specific color. He suggests that, when you speak, you are expected to "wear" that perspective:

- White hat – facts/data: Present and assess the information available, notice what can be learned from it and what additional information may be required and how it can be obtained.
- Red hat – intuition, gut feeling or emotion: Present ideas, feelings and hunches without explanation or justification. Also identify how other people may react emotionally to what is being discussed or proposed.
- Black hat – what could go wrong, a devil's advocate: Identify weak points, risks, or barriers. Take a pessimistic/cautious view.
- Yellow hat – positive outlook: From an optimistic viewpoint, identify the advantages, benefits and opportunities that are possible.
- Green hat – creativity: In the absence of criticism and constraints, freely explore what is possible, step outside of the box, outside of your habitual way of thinking, and propose creative solutions.
- Blue hat – overall process management: Outline the proposed process and notice when it is time to change hats and which hat may be the most appropriate. Summarize the agreed-upon results and next steps.

By having all relevant family members present and simultaneously "wearing" and "switching" hats during a family meeting, everyone gets to speak and be heard on what is important to them, without being criticized. This has the potential to improve communication, generate more creative thinking and lead to better decisions and support within the family. Everyone is encouraged to step out of their current thinking and provide input for each perspective (hat). To add some fun and to ensure everyone knows the current focus, six humorous, colorful hats can be made or purchased and everyone, depending on age, can take turns wearing the different hats and leading that specific part of the discussion.

There is no one sequence for using the hats. Generally, the process will start from a blue hat perspective outlining the issue to be discussed and the process to be followed. Then facts and relevant information (white hat) may be presented, followed by any of the other hats and finally wrapping up (blue hat) with a summary of the discussion, assigned responsibilities (with dates) and next steps.

The following example illustrates the type of comments that may be made for each hat.

Situation: Your ten-year-old daughter, Emily, wants to be a veterinarian. There is an issue about how her college education gets financed.

- Blue Hat
  - o Our objective is to find ways to finance Emily's education.
  - o We'll use the six-hat process, starting with the white hat.
- White Hat
  - o Using today's fees, it would cost $x for university.
  - o We have $y saved, which is significantly less than what we need.
- Red Hat
  - o (Emily) This is more important to me than anything else.
- Yellow Hat
  - o Providing Emily with the best education possible is critical for her future success and happiness.
- Black Hat
  - o We cannot penalize the rest of the family to meet only Emily's needs.
- Green Hat
  - o Emily can help the family next door and contribute 25% of whatever she earns to her education fund.
  - o We can save money by walking to church and the grocery store when the weather permits.
- Blue Hat
  - o We have made good progress. Now let's cycle through the different hats once more to see if there is anything else to discuss.
  - o To summarize, we have decided. . . . We will follow up on progress on a monthly basis.

5.6 PURSUING WHAT YOU VALUE

Values are principles, standards or qualities that you consider to be worthwhile, important or desirable. They're the reason why you are motivated to do things. Values most often operate at an unconscious level – deep inside – as the core or purpose in your life. You either move toward what you value or move away from what you do not value. Many people refer to this as moving toward pleasure and away from pain. When observing other people, you may be surprised to see them moving toward something that you do not value. However, in their model of the world, they see what they are moving toward as valuable.

Included in values are important yet intangible criteria such as success, integrity, spirituality, praise, honesty, safety, and so on. These highly valued criteria serve as a focal point around which your beliefs are organized. As you go through your daily life, you may focus on these intangible criteria, while others focus on tangible values such as money or possessions. However, behind the material values the intangible criteria still exist, and can be determined by chunking up – by asking the question, "For what purpose?"

Most likely you are not consciously aware of your values. You tend to go through much of your life on autopilot. Most of your values were established very early on. The values that made sense and served you well in your youth may still be driving your behaviors years later, simply because you are not aware of them and have not changed them to meet your current needs. Becoming consciously aware of your values can give you insight into why you pursue certain things or behave in certain ways. This awareness can also provide the opportunity to assess whether these values truly reflect who you are today, or whether they are values others have imposed on you.

As you mature, your values and their meanings change. Safety as a child may have meant not upsetting mommy or daddy. Does it still mean the same thing today? As an adult, you need to reassess your values and likely make different choices from a more mature perspective.

Values also have a hierarchy or order of importance that affects how you experience the world and live your life. A child who values school more than having a large group of friends will live a different life than one who places a higher value on a large group of friends.

Discovering your values

One of the easiest ways to discover your values is to look behind what is driving your emotions. For example:

- Anger. You become angry because you or someone else has violated something you value.
- Happy. You are happy because something you value is being achieved.
- Excited. You are excited because something you value has the potential of being achieved.
- Guilt. You feel guilty because you have violated one of your values.
- Sad. You are sad because something you value is not available to you.
- Fear. You are fearful of losing something you value or having it violated.

Of course, there are many other emotions. Think about some of the emotions you have recently experienced and become curious about exploring the values behind those emotions.

Identifying your important values

Knowing which values are most important to you and really drive your behavior can be useful. To discover your most important values:

1. Prepare a list of values that you think are important to you. Add to this list those values that trigger an emotion.
2. Once you have a good list, group together those values that have a similar meaning.
3. Identify the top ten values and order them from 1 to 10 (1 being most important in terms of how you live your life today). Realize that your number 1 value has the most influence, 2 second most and so on. A value ranked 8, although important, will not have a great deal of influence. You now have an ordered list of values that drive how you live your life.
4. If you would like to change the order of these values and have the value that is currently number six (call it value X) be the most important, start noticing those instances when X gets overridden by other values. In these situations, make a conscious choice to undo an action that does not value X. Focusing on X and giving it priority over other actions will, over time, move it up the list until it becomes installed in your unconscious as number 1.

For a more comprehensive approach for identifying and ordering your values, see my book *Live Your Dreams Let Reality Catch Up: NLP and Common Sense for Coaches, Managers and You* (Trafford Publishing, 2006).

Aligning values in your family

Not surprisingly, people operate from different values and have different interpretations of values. For example, I may value success and interpret it as members of my family working in harmony. You, on the other hand, may view success as honoring commitments and respecting other family members' time. Another person may interpret success as accumulating assets. If we are members of the same family, each of us may feel that the others fully understand and support our interpretation of success, until there is something critical to be accomplished. Then our values and interpretations come into conflict.

To manage diversity in a family and minimize potential value conflicts, everyone involved must recognize and understand that people have different values and interpretations of these values. Establishing and communicating overall family values, while clarifying and acknowledging individual family members' values, is an important part of effective communication and maintaining harmony within the family. Dysfunctional family systems result from conflicts in unspoken basic values.

5.7 IF YOU BELIEVE YOU CAN OR CAN'T, YOU'RE RIGHT

Beliefs are views, guiding principles, judgments and decisions about yourself, your family, your community and how the world functions. Your beliefs filter what you see, hear and feel in the world around you and as a result determine the meaning you associate with an event. Beliefs act as self-fulfilling prophecies. Your beliefs, whether they are limiting or empowering, determine your actions, which in turn verify your beliefs to be true. Over time, as you generate more evidence, your beliefs become increasingly entrenched and more real.

Beliefs operate at the deep structure level and influence the surface structure of your thoughts and behaviors. While you are aware of many of your beliefs, in general, your most influential beliefs operate outside of your conscious awareness. There are some beliefs that you view as absolute truths and never question – "that's just the way the world is!"

A change in your beliefs can have a major impact on how you live your life and the behaviors you manifest. In their book *NLP and Health* (Thorsons, 1996), Ian McDermott and Joseph O'Connor illustrate the power of beliefs with numerous references to medical cases. For example, in a typical clinical situation, about 35 percent of all cases receive as much pain relief from a placebo as from morphine – simply because the recipients believe it will work.

Beliefs hold in place the boundaries of your reality – what is and isn't possible. Once you believe in something, you tend to ignore counterexamples and accept only those situations that reinforce your belief. Beliefs and related stories create an imaginary boundary that limits you while giving you the illusion of safety and comfort. And until you push past this imaginary boundary you're not able to see it for the illusion it really is. What beliefs are you helping your children create that will determine how they will live their lives?

Believe and act as if it were impossible to fail.
– *Charles F. Kettering*

Where do beliefs come from?

Most beliefs originate from childhood. These beliefs are not based on fact; instead, they are based on a perception of events at the time they were formed. Generalizations are made on single traumatic experiences or through trial and error, forming our beliefs. We tend to accept those beliefs that bring pleasure, provide safety or avoid pain. Children respect those who play significant roles in their lives – parents, teachers, religious leaders, older siblings – taking on their beliefs and behaviors and accepting what they are told about themselves or others – "you are incompetent" or "you can achieve whatever you choose."

Many limiting beliefs are established during childhood, and often are based on a misinterpretation of the event, because children do not have all of the resources of an adult nor an awareness of all the facts.

To illustrate how easy it is to establish a core belief, consider how elephants are trained. You often see elephants restrained by only a light rope and stake. Why is it that these massive animals don't just walk away, since they could easily break the rope or pull out the stake? Simply, they have been conditioned to accept that they cannot. If they had the ability to reason, we could say they *believe* they cannot!

When elephants are young, they are tied up with a very heavy rope and stake that they are unable to budge or break. After many futile attempts, they accept that no matter what they do, they cannot break free. Although not real, this limitation restricts their future mobility, even in the face of danger.

Just as the elephants were trained, what boundaries are you helping your children accept that will limit how they live their lives?

Changing beliefs

The belief change cycle is a naturally occurring process:

- It begins with a tightly held belief. At one time, you may have believed in Santa Claus – a very powerful belief that had a major impact on your behaviors.
- New information leads you to begin to doubt this belief. As you grow older, you gather information from your friends, parents, TV and other media, and gradually you begin to question your belief about Santa Claus.
- You reach a point where you are open to believing something new. Continuing to believe in Santa Claus in the face of new information or the teasing of friends leads you to consider alternatives.
- A new belief, one that is either supported by this new information or maintains existing benefits or provides other perceived benefits, takes root. You now have a new belief and supporting strategies about Santa Claus that allows you to maintain the positive benefits (gifts) while avoiding the negative ones.

This process illustrates how you and your family members generate new (empowering or limiting) beliefs. As well, this process provides insight on how to change limiting beliefs: Identify the limiting belief, begin to doubt the belief as a result of new information and counter examples, identify an alternative belief that provides positive benefits, and focus on information that ratifies this new belief.

The Museum of Old Beliefs

The Museum of Old Beliefs, developed by Robert Dilts, is based on the belief change cycle. Anyone can use this process, and it's particularly useful for young children as it involves movement and depends on a good imagination.

1. On six pieces of paper, write each of the following:

    1. Current belief.   2. Open to doubt.   3. Museum of Old Beliefs.

    6. Absolutely true.   5. Open to believing.   4. New belief.

2. Place these pieces of paper on the floor, in the order indicated above, with about two feet separating each paper – that is, easy to step from one to the next.

3. Stand on the paper labeled "Open to doubt." Think of a belief that is currently true for you, yet you are open to the possibility that it isn't true – for instance, history is boring. Do this for several different situations. Really get into these beliefs – in your mind, see, hear and feel each one, while taking on any appropriate physiology. Anchor to this spot the idea of being open to doubt.

    After each of steps three to six, step off the paper and break state by stretching or looking around the room.

4. Step on the paper labeled "Museum of Old Beliefs." Think of a belief that at one time was true and is no longer true – for example, a belief in Santa Claus or I can't ride a bicycle. Do this for several situations. Really get into these beliefs. Anchor to this spot the idea of beliefs that are no longer true.

5. Step on the paper labeled "Open to believing." Think of something you're not quite convinced of totally but are open to believing it is true – for example, your favorite team will win the championship this year. Do this for several situations. Really get into these beliefs. Anchor to this spot the idea of being open to believing they are true.

6. Step on the paper labeled "Absolutely true." Think of something you're absolutely sure is true, there is no doubt whatsoever – for example, you love your parents. Do this for several situations. Really get into these beliefs. Anchor to this spot the idea of being absolutely certain they are true.

7. Step on the paper labeled "Current belief." Think of a belief that is holding you back from what you desire – limiting you in some way – for instance, math is difficult.

8. Step from the paper labeled "Current belief" onto the paper labeled "Open to doubt." Fully get into the experience of doubting this belief. A coach or parent can help by reframing the situation or by providing counter examples that really open the possibility of doubting this belief.

9. Step from the paper labeled "Open to doubt" onto the paper labeled "Museum of Old Beliefs." Fully experience the situation and realize this old belief no longer has any energy attached to it. It is simply something you used to believe. You can pretend to be in a museum and see this old belief behind glass, simply as an artifact that in the past had some use.

10. Step onto the paper labeled "new belief." What new belief would you like to replace that old belief with? For instance, math is useful and I am able to do it.

11. Once you have a new belief, step on the paper labeled "Open to believing." Fully experience the possibility of taking on this new belief and the benefits that will accrue to you.

12. Step from the paper labeled "Open to believing" onto the paper labeled "Absolutely true." Fully experience and feel what it's like to have this new belief.

13. Step away from all the papers to a neutral spot. Notice what is now possible and how you feel with this new belief. See yourself going forward into the future – a month, six months, a year from now – with your new belief.

14. Repeat steps seven to thirteen at least one more time. Each time you repeat step seven, begin to speak of the old belief as being in the past.

Swish pattern for changing beliefs
The following provides a different and equally useful method for changing limiting beliefs. It's based on submodalities, which form a key part of NLP co-founder Richard Bandler's approach to NLP. Many NLP practitioners know of the *swish pattern* in terms of changing behaviors. It can be adapted to work with beliefs. The following is based on Bandler's book *Get the Life You Want* (Health Communications Inc., 2008).

1. Think of something you doubt or are uncertain about. Elicit and record the visual, auditory and kinesthetic submodalities of your uncertainty.

2. Think of something you are absolutely certain of or believe strongly. Elicit and record the visual, auditory and kinesthetic submodalities of your certainty.

3. Think of a limiting belief you no longer want and a positive belief you want to replace it with.

4. In your mind, see, hear and feel the limiting belief rocket off into the distance and then snap back, only now it is in the submodalities of uncertainty.

5. In your mind, see, hear and feel the positive belief rocket off into the distance and snap back in the submodalities of certainty.

6. Repeat steps four and five (at the same time) until you have done them at least seven times. Make sure that together steps four and five take only a fraction of a second to complete. This is why it is called the swish pattern – in less time than it takes to quickly say "swish," you have completed steps four and five. Speed is essential.

5.8 OVERVIEW OF THIS CHAPTER

Figure 7: Mind map of this chapter:
Your Toolkit for Change

6.

Achieving Your Dreams

From time to time, you may feel there is a disconnect between what you are doing and what you want and value. Often this disconnect arises due to a lack of clarity on what you desire. Without clearly defined outcomes, you tend to live in the mundane and mindlessly repeat what you have done before. Typical problems with poorly specified outcomes are:

- Vagueness. Your outcome is not written down and thus evolves, often in a random pattern. It is not specific and therefore unclear as to what is to be achieved and how others can assist. There is no way to measure progress. Often a specific date for its achievement is missing. Without a clear objective and intermediate steps, there is nothing to celebrate achieving.
- Unrealistic. Your outcome sounds great, yet it is not achievable given your current resources (finances, education, network) and mindset.
- Unforeseen consequences. The consequences (ecology – effect on family, health) of achieving your outcome or related activities are not taken into account. As a result, unforeseen problems arise that drain resources and take your focus away from your original outcome.
- Lack of passion. Your outcome is something you would like to achieve. However, a clear driving passion is missing. Thus, your outcome is little more than a story that is recited at family get-togethers or other occasions.

As you may have noticed, I avoid using the word *goal*. In NLP, we prefer to refer to a goal as an *outcome*, removing some of the pressure and finality conventionally attached to the word *goal*. The Merriam-Webster Online Dictionary defines a goal as "an end toward which effort is directed," That is, you either achieve your goal or you don't. On the other hand, an outcome is defined as "something that follows as a result or consequence." Most people have great difficulty setting and achieving goals. However, we always achieve an outcome, and if it is not what we want, we can view this as feedback and make appropriate changes to obtain a more acceptable outcome next time.

Have a clearly stated, meaningful outcome for everything you do – family outing, playing with or supporting your children, exercising. How often have you not had a clearly stated outcome and, as a result, were co-opted to help someone achieve theirs. Afterward perhaps, you've "beaten up" yourself or them for being successful at your expense. Setting an outcome is the first step in the five steps for success. Each day, set at least one clearly stated outcome for the day that is in alignment with your overall outcome for you, your family or your children.

Encourage and assist your children in setting clearly stated, meaningful outcomes for school, their interactions within the family, their hobbies. Imagine the freedom they (and you) will have when they set and achieve their outcome to have their homework finished by 7:00 each evening – realizing there will be the occasional exception when a teacher assigns extra work.

> If you don't know where you are going,
> you may end up somewhere else.
>
> – *Yogi Berra*

The material in this chapter is written for an adult who wishes to identify and achieve a desired outcome. You can easily modify the following processes to assist your children or your family in identifying and achieving their desired outcomes.

6.1 SPECIFYING YOUR OUTCOMES

To be successful in life, you and your family members need to know what you want, express it clearly and succinctly and have a passion for achieving it. Outcome MASTERY and the NLP well-formed conditions are proven methods to assist you in specifying your outcomes.

	Outcome MASTERY
M	**Measurable** – How will you know if you are making progress and what must happen for you to know you have achieved your desired outcome? **Meaningful** – Is your outcome important for you? It needs to be meaningful for you, not someone else.
A	**Achievable** – Do you believe your outcome is achievable? It needs to be achievable in terms of what you believe, not what others believe. **All areas of your life** – Are you fully congruent for achieving this outcome or are there conflicts (internal or external) that you need to resolve? **As if now** – From this moment on, live as if you already have achieved your outcome. Many of us work on accomplishing our dreams and yet do not fully internalize our outcome. Become the person in your dreams *now*. Give yourself a makeover. Change your appearance – hairstyle, clothes, colors you wear – this may also mean eating differently, increasing your physical activity and associating with different people. Many famous people have lived their lives as if they had already achieved their dreams long before they became famous. Steven Spielberg, an influential film personality, was directing short films by the time he was fourteen.
S	**Simple** – Your outcome should describe clearly what you wish to achieve and should be expressed in very simple language and sentence structure. In this way, there is no confusion on the part of your unconscious mind over what needs to be done. **Specific** – The outcome, "I want more money" is simple, yet not specific. It does not specify when this to happen or how much more money. If someone were to give me one penny, my outcome would be achieved.

T	**Timed** – You must specify an exact time. Saying tomorrow or next month is not adequate – tomorrow will always be tomorrow. **Toward what you *do* want** – What you focus on is what you get. If your outcome is, "I don't want to fail," your focus is on failing. You will then notice all the signs of potential failure rather than the signs of success. Focusing on what you don't want implies that anything else is acceptable and the outcome you achieve may be worse than what you have now. Being aware of what you don't want can be useful to get you moving. To sustain this movement, you need to have something you're moving toward. Suppose your outcome is "I want to lose weight." Although, at first glance, you may think this is toward what you want, it is actually away from weight – "I don't want weight." This will fire the initial motivation. To keep you motivated, you need to have a toward outcome such as seeing yourself fit and healthy.
E	**Ecological** – Is your outcome in alignment with your values? What is the potential impact now and in the future on your family or school (external systems) and your health and well-being (internal systems)?
R	**Realistic** – Is your outcome realistic according to you? It does not have to be realistic in the minds of others. **Responsible** – Be at cause; assume responsibility for your actions and the consequences of achieving your outcome.
Y	**Yearning** – Without a real yearning or passion for achieving your outcome, it is only a series of words. Your passion will drive your activities and success. It will dominate your conversations, your thinking, your actions and your very being. To be passionate about an outcome, it must be in alignment with your values. You will fail to achieve an outcome if it is lifeless, too bland or one that someone else has imposed on you. In life, it is not necessarily the smartest or most gifted who succeed, it is those with desire.

Well-formed conditions

An outcome that satisfies the well-formed conditions will produce an effective and ecological result.

- State your outcome in positive terms.

- Specify your present situation. Before you can work on achieving your outcome, you need to know what resources you have available and where you are on the path to achieving your outcome.

- Determine the resources you need, such as skills, time, financing or education. Do you have the resources to initiate and maintain the outcome? If not, how will you get them?

  Ask for assistance and advice. Many people never achieve their dreams simply because they never ask for help. Be persistent in asking and finding those who can help you. After all, how serious are you about achieving this outcome? Colonel Sanders of Kentucky Fried Chicken allegedly asked *1,009* times before someone purchased his chicken recipe. At each rejection, he used his sensory acuity to learn and change his approach. He persisted until he was successful. Why? Because he believed in what he was doing, was fully committed and was passionate about his outcome.

- Specify your outcome in sensory-based terms. What specifically do you want? How will you know you if you are making progress or have achieved your outcome? Where, when and with whom will you achieve your outcome? What will you see, hear, and feel?

- Make your outcome compelling. Determine what has stopped you from achieving this outcome in the past. Is it too big or small for you?

  o Chunk down if the size of the outcome overwhelms you. If your outcome is too big, you may not know where to start, or you may nibble at the edges without making any real progress.

  o Chunk up if you find the chunks too boring or easy to accomplish. Ask yourself, "What will this outcome obtain for me or allow me to do?" Obstacles will disappear if you link your outcome to something that is important to you.

- Determine if your outcome is within your control. Is it something you can initiate and maintain yourself? The more your outcome depends on other people, the less control you have, and your chances of success diminish accordingly.

A well-formed outcome is not about other people changing. It is about changes in you that may result in a change in their behavior. An outcome such as, "my children will spend more time with me," is one that is not within your control. Consider instead, "I am, in all of my actions, beliefs and values, the type of person they would like to spend time with." Make sure this is ecological, otherwise you may feel you have given up your own needs to satisfy theirs, and they may still not spend time with you.

• Check ecology. Are there any undesirable by-products? Have you preserved the positive by-products of the current situation?

Identifying your outcomes

Many people, especially children, are not clear on what they want to accomplish, particularly in the long term. The following are two ways to shed light on your outcomes. For younger children, you may wish to make it simpler, more fun and with shorter timelines.

1. Prepare a list of your dreams:

    a. Explore different contexts such as family and friends, recreation, financial, profession, health and spirituality. Answering the following questions may help you prepare this list:

        o What do you wish to achieve in six months, one, five or ten years?
        o As you sit in your rocking chair looking back on your life, what will you say was your greatest achievement?
        o How do you wish to be viewed by family, friends and colleagues?
        o What is most important to you?
        o What brings you joy?

    b. Categorize your dreams according to family and friends, recreation, financial, profession, health and spirituality. Also identify when you would like to accomplish your dreams – six months, one year, two, five or ten years. Have dreams that are both short and long term and that cover most of the categories.

    c. Identify five major outcomes you plan to achieve. Notice that some are stepping stones to a much larger dream. Address any perceived conflicts.

    d. For each of these five outcomes, write at least one paragraph stating why achieving this outcome is important to you – include as many benefits as you can possibly think of. If, after writing the paragraphs, you find there is not a great deal of hunger, drive or passion for one or more of the outcomes, first make sure it's your outcome and not an outcome that others expect of you. Second, chunk down on those outcomes that seem too large or overwhelming or chunk up on those outcomes that seem boring or trivial.

2. Ask a special set of advisors, using the *theater of the mind*.

    Often when we ask our friends or family members for advice, although well-intentioned, the advice comes from their model of the world. Unless you have someone who is a Sponsor – as described in the next chapter – you may be better off to ask a special set of advisors, using the power of your mind and your unconscious resources:

    a. Identify three people who have the knowledge or expertise to advise you on your outcome. You do not need to personally know these people and they can be real or fictitious, alive or dead. You can change your advisors any time you need different advice.

    b. Make yourself comfortable, perhaps play some soft background music, close your eyes and journey inside to a special place called *sanctuary*. You can go to sanctuary any time you need a time-out, a place of safety to contemplate your course of action, or to get advice from your advisors.

    c. You are in charge of designing your sanctuary. In your mind, it can be anywhere you choose – next to a body of water, inside your home, or at a special vacation spot that helps you to relax.

    d. Invite your advisors into the sanctuary. Explain to them your current situation and ask for their advice on the different paths you could follow. Listen carefully, without judging, as you each ask one another questions and begin to form one or more outcomes for further consideration.

    e. Remember, you are in charge. After you fully consider all advice received from your advisors, you are the one who will make the final decision.

    f. After receiving all of the advice you need and deciding on a course of action, thank your advisors for coming and close down sanctuary until your next visit.

    g. You can go to your sanctuary whenever you desire. It can be a long visit when you just need time to relax or when you need clarity on your true desires or a short visit to quickly confirm a course of action.

Writing down your outcomes

Some people avoid writing their outcomes or setting long-term outcomes because they fear being locked into a course of action that will reduce their flexibility. Remember that outcomes can be rewritten and this process can be revisited whenever new information comes to light or a change in direction is required.

Writing your outcomes down is powerful. Reviewing what you have written, editing and rephrasing it to make it more concise and adding motivating words and action verbs allows you to clearly see your outcome, get a grasp of it and ensure that it sounds right and is ecological. This process also gives you the tastes and smells of accomplishment. This will make your outcome more real and more achievable.

1. Ensure your outcomes are described in the MASTERY format and satisfy the well-formed conditions.

2. Use the logical levels to add additional clarity to your outcome:

    • Spirituality: What is the larger system – family, community, school? How do you fit into the larger system? What is your purpose?
    • Identity: Who will you be? What is your mission?
    • Beliefs and values: What beliefs will you have about yourself and others that will make the difference in accomplishing your outcome? What about your values?
    • Capabilities/strategies: What skills and resources do you have and which ones will you need to acquire? What strategies will you use to achieve your outcome?
    • Behavior: What will other people observe about you as you work on and achieve your outcome?
    • Environment: Where, when and with whom will you achieve your outcome?

6.2 MAKING AN ACTION PLAN

You are now clear in the outcomes you wish to achieve. Your next step is to make an exciting, motivating action plan. Your plan includes your result(s), intermediate steps (milestones), reasonable time frames and an indication of the resources you will need. My suggestion is not to get too detailed as plans will change and you may find yourself planning at the expense of taking action. Indeed, when fearful of taking action some people entertain the illusion of planning to avoid taking action.

To put together your plan, you may wish to start where you are today and plan forward. Or, you can begin by assuming you have achieved your outcome and ask yourself what the step was just before achieving your outcome, and the step before that – that is, work backward. How much effort you put into your plan will depend on how big your outcome is. You may consider using the following:

1. Disney creativity strategy

    The Disney creativity strategy can be used to gain more clarity and increased passion for your outcomes. Combine this strategy with *mastermind groups* or with the theater of the mind to gain even more clarity.

2. Mastermind groups

    Mastermind groups consist of people with different interests and skills. These groups have the potential to help you see things differently, provide support and encouragement, and identify and open doors of which you may not have been otherwise aware. Mastermind groups share the basic philosophy that more can be accomplished in less time by working together. A mastermind group can be held in person, in an online chat room or on a telephone bridge conference line.

3. Theater of the mind. Use your advisors, as described above, only this time ask for their assistance in putting together a plan.

6.3 PLACING YOUR OUTCOME INTO YOUR FUTURE

The Law of Attraction tells you to visualize exactly what you want. In this section, I suggest you do more than visualize. Use all of your senses to put a compelling representation of your outcome in your unconscious mind. This strengthens your desire and persistence because you momentarily experience the thrill of having achieved your outcome. At an unconscious level, this assists you in identifying and taking advantage of opportunities as they arise. The more precisely you focus in your mind, the better the Law of Attraction works.

The following will help you "program" your unconscious mind to achieve your desired outcome.

1. Be sure your outcome is stated using the MASTERY outline.

2. Identify the last step – what is the last thing that has to happen so you know you have achieved your outcome?

3. Make an internal representation of the last step. Be fully associated by looking through your own eyes. Adjust the submodalities to enhance the positive feelings – make the final step as real as possible.

    a. Make the picture larger or smaller, brighter or darker, focused or unfocused, in color or black and white, closer or farther away, framed or unbounded, different locations (e.g. immediately in front of you or off to one side). Maintain those qualities that make your outcome the most compelling.

    b. Introduce sounds. These sounds may be someone speaking to you, music or something you are saying to yourself. Adjust the quality of the sounds by making them louder or softer, faster or slower, higher or lower in pitch, more or less rhythmic, all around or from a specific direction. Maintain those qualities that make your outcome the most compelling.

c. Introduce feelings. These feelings may be of success, well-being, love, etc. Adjust the qualities of the feelings by making them stronger or softer, in a particular part of your body or all throughout your body, constant or intermittent. Maintain those qualities that make your outcome the most compelling.

d. If appropriate and if they make your outcome more compelling, introduce tastes and smells and adjust their qualities as well.

e. Take a moment to fully enjoy accomplishing your outcome. From this moment on, live your life as if you have already achieved it!

f. If you have not already done so, take on a physiology that reflects having achieved your outcome. This will reinforce the images, sounds and feelings you have created in your mind.

4. Once the submodalities have been adjusted, view the internal representation from a dissociated perspective – you are now able to see yourself in the internal representation. An associated future outcome gives you the feeling that you have already achieved the outcome, and it therefore will not be as motivating.

5. Take the internal representation in your real or imaginary hands and begin to float out of your body and imagine yourself floating up in the air.

6. Energize the internal representation with four deep breaths – breathe in through your nose, out through your mouth, and as you exhale, imagine all of the energy from your breath flowing even more life into the internal representation.

7. Float out into the future, until you are over that future time when this event will occur. When you are over that future time, release the internal representation and see it gently float down and become part of your future.

8. Once the internal representation becomes part of your future, notice that events realign themselves between the present and this future time. Furthermore, this realignment extends far out into the future, supporting the achievement of your outcome and providing ensuing benefits.

9. Float back to the present and then down to your body. Fully immerse yourself in enjoying the benefits of achieving your outcome. Your unconscious mind does not differentiate between what is imagined and what is real.

6.4 TAKING ACTION THROUGH PERSISTENT STEPS

You must persist or your dreams will evaporate into thin air. It is well known that those who take immediate action are much more likely to be successful.

Twenty years from now you will be more disappointed
by the things that you didn't do than by the ones you
did do. So throw off the bowlines. Sail away from
the safe harbor. Catch the trade winds in your sails.
Explore. Dream. Discover.

— *Mark Twain*

Maintaining your focus

Your first action is to find a way to remind yourself every day and throughout
the day of your desired outcome. This can be something that you see, hear or
touch. My suggestion is to have both visual and kinesthetic stimuli. The visual
stimulus can be a picture, collage of pictures or clay model of your desired outcome. Position this where you can easily see it every morning when you first
wake up. The kinesthetic stimulus is something that you can easily carry in your
pocket or use as a piece of jewelry. Choose something that, whenever you touch
it, reminds you of your desired outcome.

Energy is the essence of life. Every day you
decide how you're going to use it by knowing what you want and what it takes to reach
that goal, and by maintaining focus.

— *Oprah Winfrey*

Following a program of continuous incremental improvement

To achieve your outcome, you don't have to know every step in advance. For
example, if I were traveling by car from Boston to Los Angeles, it would be useful to have some idea of the cities and states that I may drive through. However,
the most important part is to safely navigate down the next mile of highway
and ensure that my near-term actions are contributing to arriving safely at my
destination.

Same idea for achieving an outcome. You need to know your result(s) and some
possible intermediate steps (milestones), while focusing on what needs to be done
today to move toward your desired outcome. Breaking your outcome into smaller
achievable pieces allows you to take action and make progress each day.

Process for continuous incremental improvement

1. Your outcome is stated in the Outcome MASTERY format.

2. Each week, review your progress, determine if corrective action is required,
   work out exactly what you want to accomplish (outcome/s) for the coming
   week (taking into account the next milestone, even if it's several months

away). This will bring structure to your week and you'll have clarity and purpose about your life. To help you stay the course, have a support person or group with whom to review your progress.

3. On a daily basis:

- When you first wake up:
  o Notice the picture of your desired outcome. Briefly close your eyes and see, hear and feel yourself achieving this outcome.
  o Recall your outcome for this week. Decide on a minimum of three activities (no matter how big or small) you will undertake during the day that move you toward your outcome. Write them down, together with what you intend to achieve as a result of doing them. Plan these activities into your day, preferably early in the day rather than leaving them to the last moment. Undertake these activities to the best of your ability.

- At the end of the day:
  o Review how successful you were in undertaking the activities that you planned. Celebrate your successes. For those activities that did not turn out as planned, treat those results as feedback. Remember, there is no failure, only feedback. Use this feedback to decide if your planned outcome for the week needs adjusting or if you need to adopt a new approach to undertaking certain activities. Perhaps instead of doing everything yourself, you can ask others who have the skills, knowledge or time for advice or assistance. Achieving your outcomes requires that you keep at your improvement each day with relentless determination.

4. At the end of the week, review your progress:

- When you achieve an outcome, or even an intermediary step, take time to enjoy the satisfaction of having done so. Absorb the implications of your achievement, and observe the progress you have made toward your larger outcomes. Celebrate your successes. All of this helps you build the self-confidence you deserve.
- For those situations where you were not as successful as you wished, notice what new information you have and plan accordingly. Based on your achievements and feedback from the week, assess if your desired outcome needs modification and modify as appropriate.

5. Repeat the process for the next week(s) until you have achieved your desired outcome.

> We visualized what we wanted our company to
> be when it was done and every day we evaluated
> our actions and whether we were closer to the goal
> because of them.
> – *Tom Watson Sr.,* the first president of IBM

Imagine what your life would be like today, if one year ago you had worked on three action items each day to bring your dreams to life.

6.5 TAKING RESPONSIBILITY FOR YOUR ACTIONS

Have an attitude that you create whatever happens – positive or negative. And if you create it, you have the power to change it if it does not support who you choose to be.

You are the only person responsible for your actions, behaviors, thoughts, emotions, health, wealth, happiness, inner peace . . .for your life! Your thoughts and subsequent actions create all these elements of your life. Everything that has already happened in your life, you created. Everything that is happening, you are creating. Everything that will happen, you will create. Blaming, complaining or holding others responsible is giving your power away.

Rather than being a victim, you can take action and take charge of your life. You can change anything you want in your life by simply shifting your awareness and changing your thoughts.

Accepting that you create whatever happens is being at cause as opposed to being at effect (being a victim).

6.6 ESTABLISHING FAMILY OUTCOMES

The above processes can be modified to assist your family in identifying and achieving desired outcomes. It can be a great exercise to bring a family together. For example:

- Your family identifies the overall family outcomes. Through negotiation, family members clarify and accept the contribution each family member will make to support the family outcomes.
- For younger children or just to make it more fun, instead of floating out into the future, family members can imagine they are in a time machine that will take them to different times. In this way, each family member can experience the results of their actions and those of other family members.

6.7 OVERVIEW OF THIS CHAPTER

Figure 8: Mind map of this chapter:
Achieving Your Dreams

7.

Six Primary Parenting Roles

> Your children need your presence
> more than your presents.
>
> *– Jesse Jackson*

Parenting is the process of helping your children to 1) become aware of their potential, 2) expand their wings beyond their family and 3) perform and evolve at the peak of their abilities in a safe, supportive environment. It involves drawing out their strengths and helping them to bypass personal barriers and limits in order to achieve their personal best.

Each child is a unique individual, and each has his own schedule for growing up. At each stage of his growth, his needs and expectations from his parents will change. To meet these needs, parents take on different roles and communicate with each child according to that child's focus, style and age requirements. As a parent, you play six primary roles – sometimes two or three at the same time; at other times, one specific role may dominate. These roles correspond to the six logical levels, and they range from providing your child with the necessities of life (environment) to making him aware of his potential in a larger context than his current experience with his family or circle of friends (spirituality). Robert Dilts (*From Coach to Awakener*, Meta Publications, 2003) refers to these roles as: Caretaker/Guide (environment), Coach (behavior), Teacher (capabilities/strategies), Mentor (beliefs/values), Sponsor (identity) and Awakener (spirituality/purpose) – the terms in brackets being the logical levels.

Caretaker and guide

As a caretaker, you promote your children's development by providing safe and supportive environments free from unnecessary outside distractions. As a guide, you're familiar with the territory (at minimum, more familiar than your children) and provide guidance and direction on possible paths they can take to achieve their desired outcomes.

Coach

Traditional coaching, which is referred to here, is focused at a behavioral level. As a coach, you help your children perform to the best of their abilities by identifying and encouraging specific action steps they can take to reach a successful conclusion.

Teacher

As a teacher, you help your children develop new strategies, skills and capabilities for thinking and taking action, rather than focusing on a particular accomplishment in a specific situation. With your assistance, they discover and refine many of their unconscious competencies, making these a way of life.

Mentor

In the mentor role, you provide guidance and influence to generate and strengthen important beliefs and values for your children, and you function as an appropriate role model.

Sponsor

Being a sponsor, you recognize, acknowledge and promote an attribute or identity that is already within your children, but that is not yet fully apparent or that they are not yet aware of. You do not have to be a role model; you may not have the same skills as the attribute being sponsored.

Awakener

As an awakener, you bring to your children's attention something larger than themselves (family, community, spirituality) and the purpose/vision that is awaiting them.

Each of the above roles includes follow-up on your children's progress by providing respectful and timely feedback. This feedback includes praise and suggestions for improvement to help them learn and grow. For example, as a coach you provide feedback with regard to the actions your children have or have not taken, while a mentor will model and provide direction on specific beliefs or values that are important.

These competencies of caretaking/guiding, coaching, teaching, mentoring, sponsoring and awakening are essential skills for supporting your children. Each of the different levels of support requires a different interaction between you and your children, as well as a different tool set. Many situations will require a combination of these competencies.

As with the logical levels, these roles have a hierarchy. The skills related to a particular role must include and also transcend the skills of all of the previous levels. That is, a teacher must have and exhibit the skills and abilities of a coach, a caretaker/guide and more. On the other hand, a guide may not possess or need to exhibit the skills and abilities of a coach.

Parenting at the caretaker/guide and coach level is mainly focused on conscious activities – where, when, with whom and what. Parenting at the higher levels involves increased use of the unconscious and hence is more often outside of conscious awareness. For example, at the caretaker/guide and coach levels, you encourage your children to become consciously competent at managing environmental factors and their behaviors. At the higher levels, you are moving to unconscious competence. That is, eventually they are able to perform an action without thinking and it becomes a way of life.

Although I am presenting ideas from a parenting perspective, the ideas and concepts in this chapter are equally valid for managers, leaders, life or executive coaches (coaches who focus on more than just behaviors) or anyone involved in supporting another person.

In the following, I discuss each of the parenting roles in more detail and suggest NLP patterns/concepts that can be used. My suggestions are only meant to serve as a guide. Use your ingenuity and thought processes to explore how these or other NLP patterns can be used, potentially with greater impact than my suggestions. For example, perceptual positions can be used by a caretaker/guide to assess the possible impact of different venues, different people attending, or different psychogeographies. Perceptual positions can also be used by a coach to assist children in gaining insights on the impact of past or future behaviors. Or a teacher could use perceptual positions to assist children in rehearsing or assessing a specific strategy from different perspectives.

7.1 CARETAKER AND GUIDE

Caretakers and guides help their children create or take advantage of environmental opportunities and identify and address environmental constraints. For example, your children need to be in the correct state for studying, both physically and emotionally. This requires regular breaks, a healthy diet, good sleep, a supportive learning environment and a positive state of mind – for both you and them.

As your children grow up, these roles will evolve. For a newborn, you are primarily a caretaker, providing all of the necessities of life. For a toddler, there remains a clear role for the caretaker – providing a safe and stimulating play area – and as a guide you help your children navigate and explore their new ever-changing environment. Even teenagers and adult children will need you to play the role of caretaker and guide; in these situations, however, it is most often by invitation.

Questions that caretakers and guides may wish to explore:

- What resources and support do my children need?
  o   Physical, emotional, financial, educational and informational.
- How will these resources be provided and by whom?
- Into what environments will my children be going?
- What information and assistance do they need to successfully navigate these new environments?
- From my experience, what useful information, roadmaps, guideposts can I share?

If your children are in a supportive and safe environment (even if not one of your choosing), a good strategy for the caretaker/guide is not to intervene and change things, unless asked for assistance. This is especially true for older children. If things get off-track or your children seem to be lost or unsure, you can provide support through guidance/information or adjusting the environment.

Basic assumptions

All of the NLP presuppositions are applicable to each of the different parenting roles. Those that are most relevant for the caretaker/guide are:

- You cannot *not* communicate. You are always communicating. Are you communicating in a way that helps your children feel safe and supported?
- Respect for your children's model of the world. Meet your children where they are. Respect their interpretation of reality. Then, if necessary, guide and support them in moving to an interpretation where they can grow and learn.
- Your children are doing the best they can with the resources available them. Foster an environment that provides the resources they need to develop in a safe, healthy manner.
- Every behavior is appropriate in some context. If your children are exhibiting behaviors that are inappropriate, provide guidance for them to understand where, when and with whom these behaviors would be appropriate.

Caretaker and guide's toolkit

A number of tools and concepts useful for the caretaker and guide have already been covered:

- Rapport. Establish an environment of trust, understanding, respect and safety for your children through the use of matching – choice of words, behavior and interests.
- Representational systems. Respect your children's preferred representational system(s) in your communication, while providing support and safety for

them to explore and enhance their abilities in the other representational systems.

- Meta programs. Identify your children's motivation traits and use these to motivate and support them in achieving their desires.
- Resource anchors. Assist your children in creating resource anchors they can access whenever they need to quickly change their mental state to feel resourceful, energetic, happy, confident, etc. In the past, a teddy bear may have been a good resource anchor, allowing them to feel safe and loved. Transfer this resource anchor to a particular way they close their hands or to a special object so they can take it to school and avoid other children making fun of them.
- Submodalities. If your children are upset about a past event or anxious about a future event, assist them with achieving a different perspective on these events by changing the submodalities associated with the pictures, sounds and feelings they're creating in their mind. They may choose to make the picture smaller, darker and farther away. The sounds could be muffled, or in Donald Duck's voice, or less harsh, and the feelings could be diminished and replaced with a state of calm.
- Metaphors. Use your children's imaginations to create a metaphor or analogy that changes their perception or guides them safely through the current situation.

Psychogeography
If you were sitting and speaking to someone who was standing – let's say towering over you – the potential exists for you to feel uncomfortable and not an equal partner in the conversation (mismatching physiology breaks rapport). In a similar manner, the geographical relationship (spatial and orientation) between two or more people has an important, often unconscious non-verbal influence on the interaction between these people.

Consider the following:

Figure 9: More intense interaction   Figure 10: Less intense interaction

In figure 9, the psychogeography will create and support a more direct or intense interaction (positive or negative). To tone it down, you may choose to move farther away, as shown in figure 10, or you may sit or stand at right angles.

Now consider the arrangement in figures 11 and 12. In figure 11, these people are more like equal partners working on a situation or issue that is out in front of them and not seen to be "owned" by either one of them. Many NLP techniques encourage the client to take the issue and view it outside of themselves. Assisting your children using the psychogeography in figure 11 would allow you to be seen as a partner in helping them resolve their issue.

Figure 11: Equal partners   Figure 12: Taking the lead

Figure 12 depicts several possible situations:

- Your child is taking the lead and you are there to support her.
- You've put your child in the lead and you are there to make sure she carries through with the action.
- You are taking the lead and your child is simply following along.

Each of these relationships has its own place. Be aware of the messages your actions are sending to your child, both in the short and long term.

You may choose to explore other situations where you have conversations with your child, for example, one person standing and the other sitting, or perhaps at a big desk or table that separates you. Are you creating the environment that best suits your intended outcome? Use perceptual positions to assess the impact of the psychogeography in these and other situations.

When having conversations with family members, remember psychogeography and pick the situation that best supports your desired outcome.

Venting
Venting is not an NLP technique; sometimes people simply need to air their issue without comment or judgment from others. Often, once your child gets the issue outside of himself, he will realize it's not as big an issue as he had thought, and on his own he is able to come up with potential solutions. As a caretaker, your role is to create a space that allows your children to freely express themselves

without interruption or the fear of being judged, criticized or having a solution forced on them. Venting should not become a way of life.

7.2 COACH

As a coach, you help your children perform to the best of their abilities by identifying and encouraging specific action steps they can take in order to reach a successful conclusion. Through attentive observation and feedback, you help your children identify their strengths to overcome self-limiting thoughts and assist them in functioning as a contributing part of the family, their circle of friends, at school and eventually as part of the community.

In this role, you let your children know what they need to do to succeed or to gain special privileges. You set it up so they can get what they want in exchange for effort. You praise them for their good work.

Basic assumptions

The NLP presuppositions that are most relevant for the coach are:

- The family member with the most flexibility of behavior will have the most influence. Being flexible in your behaviors and approaching your coaching role from different perspectives as the need arises will give you much more influence over your children's behaviors.
- Every behavior has a positive intention. If you determine the positive intention behind an unwanted behavior and satisfy it through other means, your children have the opportunity to choose other behaviors.
- There is no failure, only feedback. For both you and your children, notice what you do, and if it doesn't work out the way you intended, take it as feedback. "What can I learn from this? If, in the future, I'm in a similar situation, what can I can do that's different to potentially achieve my desired outcome?"
- Resistance in your children is a sign of lack of rapport. If your children resist manifesting the behaviors you suggest, possibly, as a coach, you have not created an environment where they feel safe.

Coach's toolkit

Following are some useful NLP tools and techniques for the coach:

- Resource anchors. Parents can help their children use anchors or triggers to assist them with quickly getting in touch with inner resources when they need to perform in an optimal manner.
- Change perceptions. Changing how your children see, hear or feel about a certain event, issue or person can change their related behaviors. Simply

adjusting the submodalities of the picture in their minds – darker, smaller or farther away – changes their perception.

- Foreground – background. Helping your children move what they have been focusing on to the background and something they have not been noticing to the foreground can greatly shift their perception and resulting behaviors.
- Perceptual positions. Assisting your children with viewing their actions from different perceptual positions can provide insights into other behaviors that may be more appropriate.
- Clear outcomes using the MASTERY format. One of the most important skills of coaching is helping your children clearly define their desired outcomes. Without something to focus on, it's impossible to know how well your children are doing, provide feedback on their progress and establish a meaningful set of rewards. For young children who are learning to walk, this may be as simple as "Let's see you walk over to Grandpa," followed by lots of praise and hugs for whatever they accomplish. For older children, this may be a written outcome with clear steps and specified rewards: "Achieve an 80 percent average next term and we'll fund and help organize a party for you and your friends." And you can add consequences for significant deviation from the desired outcome – again written down in advance.

Five-step action plan
You and your children have set outcomes. Now it's time to take the second and subsequent steps of the five-step action plan. Coach yourself and your child through each of these five steps:

1. Have a clearly stated outcome that you are fully committed to achieve.
2. Take action through persistent steps that move you toward this outcome.
3. Pay attention. Notice what you've achieved and if you are moving toward your outcome at the pace you expect.
4. Be flexible in your approach. If what you are doing isn't working, do something else.
5. Maintain positive mental (internal representations) and physical attitudes.

Appropriate feedback
Your role as a coach is to provide timely, sensory-based, unbiased positive feedback, particularly when you see your children doing something that moves them toward achieving their agreed-to outcome. For example: "I observed you doing . . . . What I liked about it (found useful, etc.) is . . . ." Notice that the focus is on what your children are doing well. From time to time, you can give your children unearned feedback that is not related to their agreed-to task. This may be in the form of a positive comment such as, "I just love who you are," or an unexpected gift.

Generally, you avoid negative feedback by encouraging your children to identify, with your assistance, "challenging situations" and to set new related outcomes and ways and means to address them. You ensure you're available to lend a sympathetic ear or helping hand if the need arises. In this way, your children learn how to create, monitor and manage their own developmental path and learn that it's okay to do new things, make mistakes and to learn from and adjust to these unplanned consequences.

The purpose of this type of feedback is to encourage flexibility and the ability to develop new behaviors in response to changing conditions. You want your children to be free from pre-established rules and processes that worked for you, perhaps some twenty-plus years ago in a different environment.

Contrastive analysis
Situations may arise where your children perform poorly or feel unresourceful in some activity, while in a different yet similar situation they perform very well or feel really good about themselves. For example, they may perform poorly on group tasks within the family and yet be great team players on their sports team. What is the difference for them with these two experiences, and what ideas, learnings and suggestions from the positive sports team situation can be used in the family situation?

Contrastive analysis compares a situation where you perform well with one where you do not achieve your intended outcome. The purpose is to identify what behaviors were different (including body language and what you pay attention to). The identified behaviors are then applied (mapped across) to the situation where you did not achieve your desired outcome, with the intention of improving your results. This approach is also very useful in comparing two strategies, each of which is simply a sequence of behaviors.

The basic steps for contrastive analysis are:

1. Identify the challenging situation in which you (or your child) do not perform or are not as resourceful as you would like.
2. Identify a similar situation in which you perform well or are resourceful.
3. Compare the two situations. What are the major differences? What do you do differently? Was the environment different? What did you learn about yourself, about others, about the world in general that is different between these two situations? What are the significant factors that make a difference in being successful? Perceptual positions can be used to give a richer perspective on the factors that make a real difference.
4. Determine how you can use this new information to behave differently in the situation you found challenging to arrive at a different and more acceptable result.

5. Rehearse these new behaviors in your mind or through actual role play. Use perceptual positions to assess the potential impact on others and possibly identify refinements to the new behaviors.

Swish pattern for changing behaviors

The swish pattern, which is based on changing key submodalities, is a useful technique to address an unwanted behavior response to a specific stimulus. Behaviors, such as a desire to bite your nails, eat certain foods, or respond unresourcefully – perhaps your reaction when asked to speak in front of a class – are often linked with a specific stimulus, trigger or cue image.

1. Identify a) a specific behavior that you want to change and b) the stimulus that starts the process – generate a picture of this stimulus. This is called a *cue picture*.

2. Generate a picture of your new self-image with the desired behavior – satisfies the positive intent of the undesired behavior. Your task now is to link the cue picture in step one with the new self-image in step two.

3. Identify at least two submodalities that, when changed, reduce your desire for the behavior in step one and increase your desire for the new self-image in step two.

    For example, you may find that reducing the brightness and defocusing the picture of the unwanted behavior reduces your desire, while increasing the brightness and improving the focus of the picture of the desired behavior makes it more compelling. The submodalities should be those that vary over a continuous range, that is, brightness, size or focus. For the rest of the process, let's assume that the critical submodalities are brightness and focus.

4. Take the cue picture and make it big, bright and clearly focused. In a corner of this picture (say the lower right-hand corner), put a small, dark and defocused picture of the new self-image and related behavior.

    You should be associated in the cue picture (you cannot see yourself in the picture). The picture of the new self-image must be dissociated to create an end state that is motivating and appealing. An associated picture gives you the feeling that you've already made the change, and therefore it will not be as motivating.

5. Make the cue picture smaller, darker and defocused as the picture of the new self-image becomes bigger, brighter and focused. Continue until the cue picture is a small, dark, defocused picture in the lower right-hand corner of a big, bright, focused picture of the new self-image. Take a moment to enjoy the feelings associated with your new self-image and the resources you now have available to you.

6. Break state.

   It's important to break state after step five. You want to create a compelling direction from the cue picture to the new self-image. If you did not break state, you would set up a cycle where the new self-image leads back to the cue picture.

7. Repeat steps four, five and six at least seven times; step five should take a fraction of a second to complete. Speed is essential.

8. Test and future pace. Think of the cue. Do you now think of the new self-image and related behaviors?

7.3 TEACHER

As a teacher, you help your children develop curiosity, rethink old ideas, explore new areas to gain fresh perspectives and develop new strategies and capabilities for taking action. The emphasis is on new learning rather than refining previous performances (behavior). As well, you help them access a positive attitude and have confidence in themselves and those they depend on. With your assistance, they enhance their ability to concentrate, deal with unplanned consequences and handle pressure by developing their physical skills and internal resources (mental maps, strategies and state management).

Basic assumptions

The NLP presuppositions most relevant for the teacher are:

- The map is not the territory. Your children have developed their own interpretation of reality. Help them challenge old ideas to discover new ways and ideas to achieve their desires.
- Your children are doing the best they can with the resources available to them. Help them develop new physical and mental resources so they can overcome perceived limitations.
- There is no failure, only feedback. Those who are successful in life use strategies that focus on answers to the question: "What do I need to learn from what has just happened so I can achieve an even better result next time?"

Teacher's toolkit

Tools and concepts that are relevant to your role as a teacher are:

- Alphabet game and walking with grace and power. These are good physical exercises that are fun for children, change their physiology and disrupt previous thinking patterns.

- Contrastive analysis. Compare a strategy that is not producing the results you want with a similar strategy that does generate those results. Your children may be very creative with regard to the visual arts, yet they may not be as creative in exploring alternative ways to communicate with their friends. Is there something they can learn by comparing these two strategies?
- Perceptual positions. The potential impact of two different strategies can be assessed by viewing the consequences from different perspectives.
- Disney strategy for creativity. A fun way to assist your children to explore and put into action their ideas from the perspective of a dreamer, a realist and a critic.
- State management. Your children's internal states are an important influence on their ability to interact with others and perform effectively. Resourceful states help them to optimize their mental and physical competence and perform with excellence. Internal states are a synthesis of both mental and physiological attributes that influence performance and stimulate unconscious processes.
- Six hats. Your children can use the six hats process to gain clarity and develop a course of action to address an issue or explore a desired outcome.

Effective learning

The next chapter, Effective Learning, provides a number of tools and concepts a teacher can use to assist children in an academic environment. These tools and concepts are equally valuable in providing your children with strategies, capabilities and mental resources for handling life issues, interacting with others, and achieving their desires:

- Representational systems. Good teachers adapt to individual learning styles of their students. Respect and utilize how your children prefer to access and process information. Help them to develop their other representational systems to have the flexibility of processing information in a different manner.
- Meta programs. Identify and utilize your children's motivation traits.
- Strategies. Effective teachers help students develop new strategies for learning, communication and life in general, as opposed to simply presenting new content.
- Visualization and mental rehearsal. Mentally practicing and rehearsing strategies for accomplishing a particular outcome enhances your children's physical capabilities and make them part of who they are.

Dock of the Bay – accessing additional resources

Every day you are presented with opportunities to make conscious or unconscious choices about how you respond to certain stimuli, behaviors or events. Most of these opportunities are minor – choosing between a glass of milk and a glass of juice. However, some are significant, and they can set in motion a pattern or path for the way you live your life. For example, if you're exhausted, how do you react to your children's tone of voice if you perceive them to be demanding? How do your children react when their teacher assigns what they see as excessive homework?

Recall the NLP presupposition that you and your children are doing the best you can with the resources available. If, when an opportunity presents itself, you or your children recognize that each of you has more resources available, you have the potential of making better choices for yourselves.

Developed by NLP co-founder John Grinder, Dock of the Bay is a great exercise to change your or your children's viewpoint and gain additional mental resources.

1. Identify a significant situation, a time in your life when you act in a less than resourceful way.

2. Imagine sitting on an imaginary dock on a peaceful lake. Feel the warm sun on your body and a soft breeze caressing your face, and note any special sounds or smells. The idea is to be in as relaxed and resourceful a state as possible as you sit on the dock.

3. Picture someone who looks and sounds like you on an island far in the distance; someone who is going through an identical situation to that in step one. Acknowledge that the person on the island could be making better choices. What resources (e.g., confidence, energy, love) do you think the person on the island could use to improve his situation?

4. Think of someone who has these resources. You do not have to know this person personally. This person could be a character in a TV show, a colleague, or anyone who truly has the required resources.

5. Step off the dock. Step into the body of the person with the required resources. Assume the posture, feelings, voice tonality and any other important characteristics of that person, and truly feel, absorb and take ownership of those resources.

6. Once you have truly assumed the required resources, return to the dock, but only as quickly as you can bring all the resources back with you. After you return to the dock with your new resources, notice that the person on the island has also acquired these resources.

7. Watch the person on the island, who looks like you, rerun the scenario/situation from beginning to end. How is that person doing? Could they use more resources? If yes, repeat steps four through six.

8. Once the person on the island is able to run the scenario from beginning to end in a truly resourceful manner, invite that person to join you on the dock. Once the person is on the dock, wrap your arms around them, hold them close and absorb the feelings. Combine both of your resources together. As the integration is taking place, you may want to tell the other person that you love and accept them, and that they are now safe.

9. Test and future pace.

Increasing your options
In addition to being more resourceful, you may wish to be consciously aware of alternative courses of action you can follow in a specific situation – for example, your child demands a new toy when you're out shopping.

1. Identify the situation.

2. Dissociate from the experience by viewing it from third position (a resourceful, independent observer).

3. Identify three different ways (strategies) for handling this situation in addition to what you usually do.

4. For each new way, experience (from first, second, third and fourth positions) how the situation would be different if you were to actually implement this approach.

5. Repeat steps three and four until you've identified three new ways that you find acceptable for the situation in question.

Circle of power
The circle of power, which is also known as the circle of excellence, was developed by John Grinder and Judith DeLozier. This exercise helps your children develop a "ring" of excellence – a resource anchor – that they can put on their finger and draw on whenever they need a mental pick-me-up.

1. Have your child imagine a circle on the floor.

2. Have him select a resourceful state that he would like to enhance – for example, confidence.

3. Have him think of a time when he was really confident. Have him create the pictures, sounds and feelings in his mind to reproduce that state of confidence. Invite him to look through his own eyes, seeing what he saw, hearing what he heard and feeling what he felt at that time. Notice that his physiology changes to reflect these internal representations. When he notices the sights, sounds and feelings reach a peak, invite him to step into the circle, while seeing all the sights, hearing all the sounds and feeling all the feelings flood into this circle, creating a powerful place of confidence.

4. Have your child step out of the circle.

5. What other resourceful state would he like to add? Perhaps being power-ful, energetic, happy, etc. Have him think of these one at a time and repeat steps three and four. He can repeat using confidence a second or third time – using different memories each time – if he really wants to build up his confidence.

6. Repeat steps three and four until he has established a very powerful state when he steps into the circle.

7. Have your child imagine this circle shrinking to the size of a ring. With his real or imaginary hands, invite him to pick up this ring and put it on one of his fingers.

8. Whenever your child needs to experience the resource states associated with this ring, he can feel it on his finger and allow those sights, sounds and feel-ings to flood every cell of his body. Or he may choose to put the ring on the ground and watch it expand to a circle. Then step into it, taking on the physiology and allowing the sights, sounds and feelings of these resources (e.g., confidence, power, energy) to instantaneously bathe every cell and be fully available to him.

Taking the edge off bad memories
Sometimes people are haunted by bad memories – being embarrassed in front of the class or abused by a trusted friend – that get in the way of achieving what they desire. The following process, which originates from Richard Bandler, makes use of submodalities and the flow of energy within your body. When you have a bad memory, you experience energy at some location in your body. This is often where the energy ends up. You also need to notice where the energy begins and how it moves from one place to the other in a circular motion. For example, you may be aware of a feeling in your stomach. If you pay attention, you may notice that it actually begins in your chest and in a circular motion moves to your stomach. The circular movement of the energy may be clockwise, counterclockwise, a forward circle or a backward circle.

1. Recall the memory that is causing problems.

2. Notice the movement of energy and the submodalities – for instance, the picture may be close, life-sized, bright, in color, and you are associated.

3. Starting with a picture at the beginning of the memory, dissociate from the memory (see yourself in the picture), move the picture farther away, reduce the size and brightness and make it black and white (using the submodalities determined in step two).

4. Jump to the end of the memory and quickly white-out the picture and remove all sounds. Break state.

5. Repeat steps three and four at least three times.

6. Bring up the original picture of the end of the memory and make the picture small (perhaps one-third the size of the original picture). Rewind the memory backward to the beginning – see yourself moving backward, hear the sound playing backward and feel the movement of energy flow in the reverse direction.

7. Break state.

8. Repeat steps six and seven at least five times. At some point, introduce circus music or something silly that is played backward in step six. The more you repeat steps six and seven and the crazier the things (visual or auditory) you introduce to run backward, the more difficult it will be for you to recall the original memory.

7.4 MENTOR

You are continually assessing, changing and adopting beliefs and values that either support or inhibit your successes in life. Beliefs and values provide the "why" and are the deeper motivations that drive you to persevere, to succeed or to hold back. Beliefs are decisions and assessments about yourself, others and the world around you (I am a worthwhile person, the world is an abundant universe), while values are principles, qualities or concepts that you view as highly desirable – integrity, safety, love, creativity. Most of your beliefs and values were established during childhood and operate at an unconscious level. That is, you follow your beliefs or satisfy your values without putting a great deal of conscious thought into your actions. Sometimes you then wonder, "Why did this happen to me?"

A mentor functions as an appropriate role model for her children, avoiding the "do as I say, not as I do" contradiction. Instead, she provides guidance and influence that generate and strengthen important beliefs and values for her children. There is an interesting story about Mahatma Gandhi, pre-eminent political and spiritual leader of India:

A woman brought her son to Gandhi and asked the revered leader to tell her son to stop eating sugar. Gandhi replied, "Please bring your son back in three weeks." She did and upon her return, Gandhi said to the young boy "Stop eating sugar." The mother was surprised and also annoyed at the three-week delay and extra effort to bring her son back and asked, "Why did you not say that three weeks ago?" Gandhi, replied, "Because at that time, I was eating sugar and I had to fully stop before advising you son to do so."

Basic assumptions

The NLP presuppositions most relevant for the mentor are:

- The map is not the territory. Your child interprets the world around him through his beliefs and values. Many of the beliefs and values that will guide him through life will come from his school environment, his religion and, most importantly, you.
- Every behavior has a positive intention. At our core, every one of us is positively intentioned. Having appropriate beliefs and values permits the results of these intentions to be expressed in a useful and ecological manner.
- There is no failure, only feedback. Occasionally, you may slip by modeling undesired beliefs and values to your children. Recognize this slip as feedback and determine how you can put the current situation right and how you can get a better result in the future. Thus, you will be modeling a presupposition that will serve your children well.
- Be the person you would like your child to be. Although not one of the regular NLP presuppositions, it certainly fits in this context.

Mentor's toolkit

Tools and concepts already discussed that are useful for the mentor are:

- Discover your values and those of your children. Which values really drive the results they achieve? Are they open to reordering the priorities of these values?
- Museum of Old Beliefs. Put beliefs that are no longer serving you or your children into the museum. Encourage them to live their lives with beliefs that support who they choose to be.
- Dock of the Bay. This highly effective exercise can be adapted to work with beliefs and values as well as resources.
- Act "as if." Are your children holding themselves back because they don't believe they can perform a certain activity or something is possible? Explore with them, "What would happen if you could do this?" or encourage them to act "as if" they can and have them identify what would then be possible. If they know someone who can perform the activity, have them role play "as if" they were that person and have them demonstrate how that person would go about performing the activity.
- Reframing. We often hold ourselves back by putting limits or frames around what's possible – we're held back by our own limiting beliefs. Stepping outside of your children's limitations as well as your own enables you to provide your children with a different interpretation that enlarges their world, providing more choice and opportunities for success.

Building a belief bridge

The following process is based on a demonstration by Robert Dilts, (April 2006, Annual Conference of the Canadian Association of NLP [CANLP], Toronto). This process can be used when beliefs get in the way of actualizing a specific identity or achieving a specific outcome (or state). The following is presented from an identity perspective. In this exercise, you see your child as more than the beliefs that have limited her up to now.

1. Ask your child, "What is the identity that you want to grow into? That is, what's the role? What would it be like to be that type of person?"

    Your child describes the role (identity) she wants to take on. For example, "I would like to be a competent student, who achieves good grades and is well-liked by my classmates." Mark the place on the floor where she stands at this moment. This will be called the current space and denoted as □.

2. Say to your child, "From what you said, you want to be (identity your child wants to grow into – use her words). Is that correct? Is there a spot on the floor that represents this identity?" Mark this spot as ☺.

3. Have your child stand on ☺ and describe what it would be like to fully become this new identity. Summarize the key points and repeat back to your child using her exact words – not your interpretation of her words.

4. Have your child move back to the current space □. Say to her, "When you're not there (point at desired state space ☺), you're here (point to current state space □), and that (point to ☺) seems unattainable. What's stopping you?"

    You need to get your child's beliefs out on the table. Until she states them clearly, all you have is an invisible barrier she keeps bumping into. By having her express this barrier in words, your child can see it for what it is and be in a position to get over it.

5. Ask her, "What beliefs do you need about yourself, others, the world, that, if you had them, you would easily get past this?"

    Your child states these new beliefs positively in the present tense: "I am . . . ." or "I am capable of . . . ."

6. Say to her, "Imagine taking those beliefs inside you, having them integrate and energize each cell in your body. Now speak those beliefs from a position of them being absolutely true."

    In her response, observe your child's voice tonality and physiology to ensure they reflect these new beliefs. If they don't, have her repeat saying these new beliefs until her voice and physiology are in alignment with the new beliefs.

7. Invite your child to stand at the current state position ☐. Say to her, "Take those new beliefs and physically and mentally bust through (with energy, feeling and appropriate physiology) what was stopping you as you move to ☺."

Have you child move forward in a powerful manner – this builds a bridge to your child's desired state ☺. Have her stand in the desired state ☺. Have her state her new beliefs from this space. Watch your child's physiology and listen to her tone of voice. Ensure she states her new beliefs in a congruent physiology and tone of voice before proceeding.

8. Have her visualize what the future will be like with these new beliefs. Identify the next smallest step she can take to maintain and energize these new beliefs and identify.

Congratulate or acknowledge your child for having the strength and courage to make this happen.

7.5 SPONSOR

As a sponsor, you assist your children to discover their mission in life. You may see something within them that they and others are not yet aware of. (Recognizing her daughter's talent, Shania Twain's mother managed to get singing lessons for Shania when she was less than five years old, even though the family could not really afford them.) You help them to establish their unique identity by supporting them in setting healthy boundaries between who they are and others. Along the way, you help them identify those core beliefs that will define who they are, while moving past beliefs that may constrain them. You do not have to be a role model and you may not have the skills your children will need to acquire. Your role is to identify and nurture your children's growth at the identity level.

Basic assumptions

The NLP presuppositions most relevant for the sponsor are:

- Respect for your children's model of the world. Your children may choose a different path than you had envisioned. Respect this choice and help them discover and live their dreams.
- The family member with the most flexibility of behavior will have the most influence. Be flexible, and think outside your own and your children's current perceived limitations to nurture and support their growth.

- Every behavior has a positive intention. Your children's behavior, even though you may find it inappropriate, has a positive intention and indicates a need or desire on their part. Help them to discover what it is.
- Your children's resistance is a sign of lack of rapport. You may see something within your children that they don't yet see; thus their resistance. This does not mean they disagree with what you have identified. It may be that they don't feel safe pursuing it at this time or you haven't created an environment of safety within which they can freely discuss and explore this possibility.

Sponsor's toolkit

Some of the tools and concepts relevant to your role as a sponsor are:

- Rapport. Create a place of safety with your children where they can freely express their dreams and concerns.
- Representational systems. People at the top of their game use all of the representational systems. Encourage your children to use each to its full advantage.
- Meta programs. Understanding what motivates your children will allow you to present your observations in a way that is motivating to them.
- Visualization and perceptual positions. Assisting your children to mentally rehearse from the four perceptual positions will provide them with valuable insights on how best to fulfill their mission.

Listening

Although related in some aspects to venting (presented under caretaker/guide), the focus here is quite different. In the former, your children need to express themselves to unload a problem or issue and get it outside of themselves so that they can see, hear or feel it from a different perspective. With you in the role of listener, it is about your children expressing thoughts on who they are and what they see their mission being, along with concerns and questions they may have. Your role is to create a space of safety where they can freely express themselves and for you to truly be there for them – a resource and a pillar of support.

To be an effective listener, relax, clear other thoughts from your mind, put your focus deep inside yourself and listen to what your children have to say while fully connecting emotionally with them. Allow them to fully express themselves, as you listen with care, with curiosity, without judgment and without offering advice unless invited to do so. Base your listening on the assumption that your children know what they need to do, they just need the resources, the opportunity and the time to discover it.

Who I Am Makes a Difference®

In 1980, Helice "Sparky" Bridges developed the "Who I Am Makes a Difference® One Minute Blue Ribbon Acknowledgement" process. (http://www.make

adifference.com/TYG/BK60.php#Helice, June 2009.) This program teaches children and adults how to show their appreciation, respect and love for one another. Reported results include: less fighting, healed marriages, increased self-esteem and improved school grades. In 1988, it was credited with preventing a boy from committing suicide.

The easiest way to explain this is to invite you to watch the six-minute video at www.blueribbonmovie.com. Then give a blue ribbon to those who are special in your life.

Building self-esteem
You can give your children a blue ribbon every day by actively acknowledging their existence and unique gifts. Use words such as: I see you, I like what I see, you are welcome here, I hear you, you are capable, you deserve this, you are valuable, you belong.

As a daily routine, you can choose to notice at least one thing your children have done well. Identify the positive intention or attribute associated with that behavior. Then tell your children how much you appreciate what they did and that they are the kind of people who are . . . (select an attribute you have identified, e.g., kind, loving).

What I want you to know
People carry with them personas or limitations that hold them back from fully expressing who they can be. The following exercise, which has its origins in work by Stephen Gilligan, will assist your child in decloaking and moving forward in his life. If both parties fully participate, this exercise has the potential to create a deep, intimate bond.

With your child, sit quietly and gently focus your attention inside your body. Then without judgment, future blame or repercussions ("what is said here, stays here"), listen as your child completes the following two sentences:

What I want you to know about me is that I am . . . .
And what I don't want you to know about me is that I am . . . .

Then you say with love and acceptance:

And isn't it great that you can be both at the same time and continue to learn and grow.

Alternate turns. Repeat about five times.

Some examples:

What I want you to know about me is that I am a fun-loving kid.
And what I don't want you to know about me is that I am afraid to disappoint my parents.

What I want you to know about me is that I am a loving parent.
And what I don't want you to know about me is that I am afraid you will not love me.

What I want you to know about me is that I am a loving parent.
And what I don't want you to know about me is that I am not sure how to show that.

7.6 AWAKENER

As an awakener, you bring to your children's attention and help them take action in something larger than themselves (family, community, country, the world, spirituality). Your children become aware of their purpose and vision and who else they have affected and will affect. This is about "stepping outside the box" – the smaller world they have created through self-imposed limitations, habits, limiting beliefs or lack of awareness of something bigger.

Like all the other levels, the skills related to being an awakener include and also transcend all the skills of the other levels that precede it – caretaker/guide, coach, teacher, mentor and sponsor. An awakener supports his children by providing contexts and experiences that bring out the best of their understanding of love, self and spirit. An awakener "awakens" his children through his own integrity and congruence and through being fully connected to his own personal vision and mission. Awakening your children involves the unconditional acceptance of who they are and at the same time, includes the suggestion that there are possibilities for expansion and evolution. An awakener can only awaken others to something larger if he is already awakened to it.

> There are two lasting bequests we can give our children.
> One is roots. The other is wings.
> – *Hodding Carter, Jr.*

Basic assumptions

The NLP presuppositions most relevant for the awakener are:

- The map is not the territory. A larger territory is out there that your children have not even begun to map. Introduce them to this larger world.
- Children do the best they can with the resources available to them. In a larger world, your children will have many more resources and opportunities available to them.
- Every behavior has a positive intention. Perhaps your children are demonstrating behaviors that are pushing the bounds of their current world, and it's time to introduce them to something much more expansive.

Awakener's toolkit

Aligning logical levels for personal congruence, presented earlier, is a useful exercise to align your actions, strategies, beliefs and values with your role as awakener.

Other tools and concepts are:

Create a state of not knowing
Once a question is answered, it locks in the response as being absolutely true and no further exploration or learning is achieved. Create a number of questions about yourself, your family and the world in general. Use these questions to gather information. Never consider the questions fully answered. As you gather information, use this new information to generate even more questions.

Avoid making assumptions or settling on answers that limit what is possible for you and others. Don't put yourself or others in a box. Avoid assigning labels and assuming you know. Avoid the stories that lock in the past, establish artificial boundaries and make moving forward difficult.

Encourage your children to do the same and share what each of you has discovered.

Vision quest
Although usually associated with Native American traditions, vision quests have been practiced around the world – religious pilgrimages, mythological tales and our own pursuit of truth and purpose. For Native American groups, vision quests may last several days. During this time, the child is attuned to the spirit world and a guardian animal will often come in a vision or dream, and the child's life direction will appear at some point.

You can go on a multi-day vision quest or obtain many of the same benefits by simply putting your work, commitments and other issues aside, asking a question you'd like to explore and then going for a nature walk at your own pace.

Former Canadian Prime Minister Pierre Trudeau is known for his famous "walk in the snow." After taking his sons to judo and putting them to bed, he decided to go for a solitary walk in a major snowstorm. This walk allowed him to clear his mind and gain clarity on what he would do next with his life. The next morning, he announced his resignation as Prime Minister of Canada. He said that during the walk he looked for destiny in the sky and listened to his heart.

During our NLP practitioner trainings, we ask all students to physically partici-pate in an exercise called Eagle Peak (Eagle Peak is our name for a substantial hill located near our training center). You can use any form of a nature walk.

1. At the bottom of Eagle Peak, ask yourself a question on which you would like to gain more information or insight. This might be an issue that is currently bothering you.

2. Put the question aside, clear your mind and begin climbing Eagle Peak as you best see fit.

3. Pay attention to what you notice and are aware of as you climb. Is there symbolism, a message, in what you experience or don't experience with your senses?

4. Keep the experience playful!

5. What do you notice that you may not have been aware of before?

6. Create your "peak" experience by standing in silence for a few minutes at the top and expanding your awareness all around you. Let thoughts and insights flow.

7. As you make your way down Eagle Peak, pay attention and notice what else is available.

8. Take time at the bottom of Eagle Peak to consider what really stood out during your journey. Is there a message in the form of symbolism or metaphor that can enrich your understanding of your question?

Addressing double binds
A double bind has the potential of putting your child in a no-win situation. Consider the following story.

A boy comes home from school and immediately goes to his room to do his homework. His father sees him and tells him he also needs to be outside getting fresh air and exercise. The next day his father sees his son outside playing with his friends and says he should be inside making sure his homework is done. The boy gets frustrated, and the father tells him he really needs to take more responsibility for his actions and pay attention to what needs to be done.

The double bind the boy finds himself in is:

1. If you're doing your homework, you should be outside getting exercise (thus you are not meeting my expectations).

2. If you are outside, you're not doing your homework (thus you are not meeting my expectations).

In addition, the source of the problem is presented as the boy's inability to take responsibility for his actions rather than his father's lack of clarity.

Double binds can put your children into a position of "damned if you do and damned if you don't." To avoid putting your children into a double bind, create a positive double bind by validating your children no matter what they do. If they are stuck or undecided about a choice they have to make, be clear (voice tonality, physiology) that no matter what their choice, they are okay and have your full support.

Robert Dilts (*From Coach to Awakener*, Meta Publications, 2003) presents a process for transcending double binds to find alternative ways of proceeding.

1. Recall a situation where you feel you're in a double bind.

2. Move your attention to that of an independent observer (third position) who is seeing and hearing the situation in step one. That is, you are dissociated from the original experience. From this perspective, are there any new learnings that provide you with different choices?

3. Move your attention from that of the observer to a place behind the observer, observing the observer. In this way, you're creating a greater degree of dissociation. Notice and record any new learnings from this perspective.

4. Repeat step three several more times – creating even more dissociation as you become the observer of the observer of the observer, and so on. As Dilts says, you get a kind of spiritual perspective and get "God's thoughts" on the situation.

5. Retrace your steps, one observer at a time, bringing all of your new learnings with you. Finally, re-enter your body and notice that with these new learnings your experience of the original situation is quite different, giving you many other choices.

Stepping outside of the box
The following is a fun exercise to help you and your family members to think outside of the box. It will also assist your family in getting new insights on how to resolve an issue.

Decide on an issue or something that you and your family would like to get a different perspective on. Then randomly select a page in the dictionary, place your finger randomly on the page and notice the first noun. I suggest you avoid nouns that you cannot touch in physical time and space – for instance, love, relationship, leadership. As an individual or team, what are some of the attributes of this noun that could apply to the problem you're working on? For example, if the word is *tree*, what attributes does a tree have that could be useful in this situation – for instance, grounded, strong yet flexible.

To make it easier and more fun for the younger members of your family, identify the names of one hundred animals, plants and objects that everyone is familiar with. Write these names on separate pieces of paper and then draw one at random.

Get out of your comfort zone – this is where learning takes place.

7.7 CHOOSING WHICH ROLE TO USE

Often it's obvious which role to use as a parent:

• Guide your toddler to move safely around his home.
• Provide coaching when he is not sure what to do.
• Teach him certain skills or how to do something.
• Act as a role model.
• Sponsor a unique ability.
• Help him become aware of a larger system and the impact he has on this system.

Other times it's not as obvious. For example, let's say your child comes home from school and says, "I can't learn math in Mr. Brown's class." What role do you play? It depends on where your child is placing his emphasis. In a situation such as this, get curious, create a space of safety so he can freely express himself and explore what he means by this statement.

Here are some examples. If your child's focus is on:

• Mr. Brown's class – it's about creating a better environment for learning (caretaker/guide).
• Math – a particular behavior – he needs coaching on what to do.
• Learning – a capability – he lacks the skills or doesn't know how to learn and needs a teacher to provide assistance.
• I can't – a belief that limits him – as a mentor assist him with addressing this belief.
• I – which resonates at the identity level – he needs a sponsor to assist him in discovering what he is not aware of about himself.
• The larger purpose in learning math. Awaken your child to the benefits of learning math and how it is important in a larger system than, say, his school.

7.8 OVERVIEW OF THIS CHAPTER

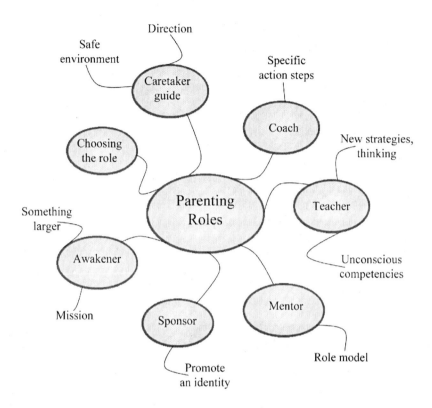

FIGURE 13: MIND MAP OF THIS CHAPTER:
SIX PRIMARY PARENTING ROLES

8.

Effective Learning

The human brain is very complex and capable. Far too often it is used simply as an information storage and retrieval device. Neuroscientists have shown that the human brain can change structurally and functionally as a result of learning and experience. Positive, supportive and stimulating environments encourage the development of new neural connections for learning, remembering and problem solving, no matter what your age. Such environments are often the opposite of the dull and rigid environments some children are subjected to at school. This leaves a major function for parents to undertake.

Many people refer to the material covered in this chapter as *accelerated learning*. For me, it's not just a matter of making the learning process faster, it must also be effective, efficient and fun. I have chosen to call this chapter *Effective Learning*, following the Merriam-Webster dictionary's definition of *effective* as "producing a decided, decisive, or desired effect," and listing the word's synonym as *efficient*.

> Learning is not a spectator sport.
>
> – D. Blocher

8.1 PARENTAL ROLES

To recap, you take on many different roles supporting your children as they develop their learning capabilities:

- Caretaker/guide. Your caretaker role is to ensure your children have a supportive, safe, stimulating and healthy learning environment at home and at school; indeed, anywhere they will be exposed to new ideas, concepts or challenges. This includes regular breaks from studying, a healthy diet, a good night's rest and a place where it's safe to make mistakes, while reasonable expectations are established and upheld. As a guide, you have experience with learning environments or are prepared to inform yourself about them.

With this knowledge in hand, you provide timely and effective advice as your children navigate these environments with your assistance or on their own.

- Coach. As your children develop their learning skills, they need to be coached on setting and achieving clear, motivating learning objectives, taking action, monitoring progress and responding with appropriate corrective action.
- Teacher. Learning is a process. As a teacher, you help your children discover how they learn best, develop valuable skills for learning and adopt effective learning habits (strategies).
- Mentor. Effective learners have a strong, supportive collection of beliefs and values about themselves and the whole learning process. Your role is to identify and nurture those that are most appropriate for your children.
- Sponsor. As your children develop and grow, they may not be fully aware of their innate strengths and capabilities. Your role is to sponsor their development by identifying those that support their true and desired potential.
- Awakener. As an awakener, your role is to raise your children's awareness of what else is possible in a world beyond their family, school and community for which their skills and abilities are ideally suited. Provide a purpose that is reasonable, engaging and motivating for your children.

8.2 CONCEPTS YOU ALREADY KNOW

The following is a quick recap of some concepts already covered. For concepts not mentioned, you and your children are only limited by your imagination and desire to explore alternative ways of achieving each of your outcomes.

- Rapport. By matching your children's physiology, tone of voice and choice of words, you create a comfortable environment to work together. For example, if they are sitting down, avoid standing over them. Also be fully present and not working on other things if you have agreed to help them.
- Psychogeography. When assisting your children, be aware of where you sit or stand in relation to them.
- NLP Presuppositions. They are all important. Five that are particularly relevant are:
  o Respect for your children's model of the world.
  o The family member with the most flexibility of behavior will have the most influence.
  o The meaning of communication is the response it gets.
  o There is no failure, only feedback.
  o Everyone does the best they can with the resources available to them.
- Chunking. To more easily remember a list of items, group similar items together and assign a name for each group. When it's time to remember the items, first recall the group names, then the items within each group.

- Anchors. Create resource anchors for your children to recall those feelings that support them in learning – e.g., calm, confident, resourceful and curious.
- Address limiting beliefs.
- Reframe. Provide a different interpretation or meaning of a situation or behavior (your children's or someone else's) that supports them in moving forward in a positive manner with their studies.
- Precision questions. Use precision questioning to help you and your children gain clarity on exactly what the issue is.
- Embedded commands, double binds and metaphors. Use these language patterns to assist your children in feeling better about themselves, accomplishing certain tasks or seeing the world differently.

Establish an outcome for learning

An explicit outcome provides your children with a clear idea of what they are moving toward and how you can be of assistance. If your children don't have an outcome for learning and if you don't have an aligned outcome in supporting them, each of you will put in a great deal of effort, experience a great deal of frustration and really not accomplish a lot.

Use the MASTERY format to establish outcomes for you and your children that you all agree on for the short (this week) and long term (this semester or longer). If your children have a clearly established outcome for their future, so much the better, as this provides a context and motivation for what they will be learning. Be sure to link their outcome to something they value to ensure they're motivated and passionate in achieving it. Find a way to link your children's school experience to their larger outcome in life.

8.3 IDEAS TO CONSIDER

The following will assist your children in improving their learning abilities:

- Children remember better if they're refreshed, focused and alert. This suggests short concentrated study sessions with quick breaks in between.
- They tend to remember information that is unusual in some way, is repeated or is at the beginning or end of a presentation or study session. The decay of memory is such that an hour after memorizing information, approximately half of the information may have been forgotten. A day later most of the information may not be recalled.
  o Have your child study for twenty minutes and then take a five minute break. During the break, have her do something fun and energizing that gets her blood flowing and carrying nutrients and oxygen to her brain.

o   At the end of each twenty-minute session, have her review the key points (highlights) in the material covered.

o   At the beginning of the next twenty minutes, have her quickly review the key material from the previous study session. Identify possible new key points to pay attention to during this study session.

o   To put information in long-term memory, have her review a couple of hours later, then in a couple of days and then in a couple of weeks.

- New habits (strategies) for learning become a way of life if they're consistently performed for five to thirty days.

- Your child's mind handles mental images of real things, especially vivid and unusual ones, far more effectively than words, numbers or abstract concepts. To create a strong memory, have your child store the information using as many senses as possible. The information she gathers through her different senses is processed in different parts of her brain. By the time she has pictured it, heard it, done it and, if appropriate, gained a taste and a smell for it, then she's made sense of it!

- Georgi Lozanov, psychiatrist and educator, and others have discovered that background music, particularly classical and baroque, can enhance learning (Georgi Laozanov, *Suggestology and Outlines of Suggestopedy*, 1978, Gordon and Breach). Research indicates that the rhythm and mathematical characteristics of baroque music synchronizes both the left and right hemispheres of your brain. This synchronization leads to a relaxed body and alert mind – ideal states for optimal achievement. Mozart's work is most often associated with enhanced learning. Other baroque composers are Handel, Bach and Vivaldi.

- Current research indicates that 50 percent of your child's brain's nerve cells are connected by the age of six. These connections form the foundation for future learning. Furthermore, ages six to twelve are the most formative years for developing basic skills. During this early development, children are in school, yet they will spend more time interacting with their family. This implies that family, not school, is the most significant learning environment and that you, their parent, play a more important role than teachers. Your task is to create a mutually supportive bridge between home and school.

- Sleep is essential to learning. Staying up all night to cram for a test does not pay off. In an experiment, participants, who were allowed to sleep on the night after participating in a training program, performed the task better the following day. They showed further gains over the next three days. In contrast, participants deprived of sleep on the night after training didn't perform the task better the next day. They showed little improvement even when allowed to catch up on their sleep over the next two nights ("Visual discrimination learning requires sleep after training," Robert Stickgold, *Nature Neuroscience*, December 2000, pp. 1237–8).

8.4 FIVE STAGES OF LEARNING

There are five different stages of learning:

Stage 1: Unconscious incompetence
This is the domain of "you don't know you don't know." For example, your child sees his older sibling easily riding a bicycle. Never having done it before, he thinks, "That looks easy. I can do that." That is, he is not aware of the skills required to ride the bicycle and that he doesn't have those skills at this time.

Your role is to assist your children in becoming aware of their deficiencies by demonstrating or informing them of the required skills and the ensuing benefits, thus assisting them to move to the next stage of learning.

Stage 2: Conscious incompetence
Your child is now aware of his current limitations in a certain area (e.g., riding a bicycle) and the importance of acquiring these skills and competencies. He realizes that by improving his skills his effectiveness will improve. Ideally, he makes a commitment to learn and practice the new skills, and eventually moves to the next stage of conscious competence.

Teachers and parents often make the assumption that children are at this stage (conscious incompetence), when they are actually at stage 1 – totally unaware of their incompetence – and thus unaware of the need to learn this new skill. Stage 1 must be addressed before moving to stage 2.

Stage 3: Conscious competence
Your child has now acquired the skills and can ride his bicycle; however, he has not fully mastered these skills and it takes his full concentration to reliably complete the task at hand. This is very much a conscious activity. Practice is required to become unconsciously competent with this new skill.

Stage 4: Unconscious competence
The skill is now a way of life and your child can easily ride his bicycle while talking to friends or adjusting his clothing. He performs this skill without even thinking about it. It becomes second nature, an unconscious activity. If a friend asks your child to teach him how to ride a bicycle, although very skilled, your child may not fully know how he does it.

Stage 5: Conscious unconscious competence
Not only has your child mastered the skill, he also consciously knows how he does it and can instruct others in doing it as well.

8.5 LEARNING STATE

Being anxious or fearful is not conducive to learning. Yet, often your child may consciously talk himself into these states based on past experiences. To be an effective learner of academic material, a quiet, calm and focused state is required rather than a hyped-up, energetic one. The relaxed yet alert alpha brainwave state is most appropriate for effective learning. Some children naturally enter this state whenever they need to process lots of information, others achieve it through meditation or daydreaming.

Accessing the learning state

- To the best of his ability, encourage your child to clear his mind of any chatter.
- Have him find a spot on the wall in front of him that is above eye level and focus his attention on this spot.
- While focusing on the spot, slowly have him expand his focus to include objects and actions in his periphery, while still seeing the spot on the wall. He should expand his peripheral vision as far as possible.
- After about twenty seconds, he should begin to notice a state of relaxation come over him. Instruct him to allow this relaxation to go to every cell in his body. He is now in the learning state.

Some children, when they do this for the first time, think they have to sit or walk like zombies. This is not true. Your child can go about his normal activities while maintaining peripheral vision. Not only will this state allow him to take in and process more information, it creates a state of relaxation and minimizes unwanted emotions such as fear and anxiety. Peripheral vision is used by many good trainers and presenters to access a state of relaxation and heightened awareness. Peripheral vision is the opposite of foveal vision, which is the highly focused vision of fight or flight.

8.6 OFTEN THERE IS MORE THAN ONE WAY TO LEARN

Often there's more than one way to learn, and you need to support your children's preferred learning style. Even if you were highly successful getting through your own school years in your way, your children will enjoy and be more successful with a process that supports their particular learning style. Having said that, there are exceptions that you and your children should pay attention to. For instance, good spellers use a visual strategy.

Motivation

Your motivation for learning may be quite different from those of your children. Identify the meta programs that motivate your children in a learning situation and find ways to enhance their motivation.

- **Toward – Away From**
  Toward learners will be motivated to learn if the material will help them achieve what they desire in their life at the moment. Away From learners

will be inclined to learn those concepts that will allow them to fix what they perceive is broken or wrong.

- **Internal – External**
  If your children have a preference for Internal, they will already know if they are doing a good job learning the material. Saying, "I know you are doing well," in a situation where they have decided they are having difficulty will most likely be greeted with an emphatic, "No, I'm not!" Here, you need to acknowledge their opinion and let them know you're available to help when they decide they need it.

  Children with an External frame of reference will decide if they're doing well based on what others say. A well-intentioned teacher or parent may suggest areas for improvement without letting them know they're already doing very well. In this case, given the only feedback that they receive is about improving, they will assume they are not doing well. Give these children lots of supportive feedback.

- **Options – Procedures**
  Options-oriented learners are continually exploring different ways to learn, and they learn best by exploring an idea from different perspectives. In so doing, they may never finish what they started. In some situations, they may need a little encouragement such as, "Once you complete this, you'll have the freedom and new knowledge to explore other ways to achieve what you really want."

  Children with a preference for Procedures will be lost if they do not have a clear process or procedure to follow. They will be upset if you suggest a way that's different from what their teacher outlined.

- **Proactive – Reactive**
  Proactive children rush ahead to get their lessons done. And they may be done without a great deal of planning or waiting for instructions. Here you may wish to point out (particularly if your children also have an Away From tendency) that with a little planning, they can avoid unnecessary problems and actually get more done in the same amount of time.

  Reactive children will delay, hoping to gain a better understanding before undertaking the assignment. You may have to prod your children by reminding them that they had ample time to reflect and now they need to take action.

- **Sameness – Differences**
  Children with a Sameness pattern will learn by noticing what is the same as or similar to something else they have learned. Children who sort for Differences will look for what is different.

Visual and other learning preferences

The representational systems form the base for four learning preferences or styles – visual, auditory, kinesthetic and auditory digital. You use all four of the learning styles to some degree. Your children's preferred learning style is a habit or strategy that is based on their preferred representational system.

- Visual. Learn by seeing it – reading, pictures or diagrams, demonstrations or watching videos, eventually picturing it in their mind.
- Auditory. Learn by hearing or saying it – CDs, lectures, debates, discussions, and verbal instructions.
- Kinesthetic. Learn by getting a feel for it – physical involvement, hands-on, moving or touching.
- Auditory digital. Learn by figuring it out, making sense of it – facts and figures and logic.

Lynn O'Brien, Specific Diagnostic Studies, Inc., found that about 40 percent of people have a preference for a visual learning style, 15 percent for auditory and 45 percent for kinesthetic (Dee Dickinson, *Learning Through the Arts*, New Horizons for Learning. Seattle, 2002, www.newhorizons.org/strategies/arts/dickinson_lrnarts.htm. Accessed June, 2009). Unfortunately, I have not seen statistics that have included auditory digital, which usually gets grouped with auditory. Since most of the information in traditional classrooms is presented orally, there is a high probability that your children will need assistance learning outside of school. Kinesthetic learners may have additional difficulty in school, as moving around is often associated with slacking off or not paying attention.

As a parent, you can use two complementary activities to support your children in learning effectively:

- Determine your children's preferred learning style. Presenting information that is in alignment with their preferred learning style will make learning easier and more enjoyable.
- Gently introduce your children to the other learning styles so they can take advantage of information available through these channels. Depending on the context, some learning styles are better than others. To be an effective learner, your children need to be comfortable in moving from one learning style to another. Ensure your children avoid thoughts such as, "I'm visual (or auditory, etc.) and so can't learn with the other modalities." This instills an excuse or self-limiting belief that gives them permission not to achieve certain things.

Suggestions for augmenting learning styles

No matter what your child's preferred learning style, she can use the following suggestions to enhance or develop each of her learning styles.

Visual
- Use pictures, photos and color to highlight main ideas in your notes, text-books, handouts, etc.
- Create pictures in your mind or on a piece of paper that illustrate what you're learning. Mind maps – diagrams used to represent words, ideas, tasks or other items linked to and arranged around a central key word or idea – are used at the end of each chapter of this book to help you remember what you've read. The funnier, weirder or more colorful the picture, the more you will remember.
- Before reading a chapter of a book, briefly preview it by looking at the illustrations, section headings, etc., and form a picture that you can further develop as you get more information.
- View demonstrations and videos to see how something is done.
- To develop an idea, draw it in the form of symbols, charts and diagrams.

Auditory
- When someone is speaking, notice the different voice tonalities and how these emphasize or de-emphasize the point they are making.
- Discuss the key information presented in charts, diagrams and pictures with someone else so you can hear other points of view.
- Summarize your notes and say them to yourself out loud or hear them spoken in your mind.
- When reading a book, if there is dialogue, hear how that person would say those words, given the context.
- Ask lots of questions.

Kinesthetic
- Get a feeling for what you're learning through hands-on experience (participating in exercises) or acting out various roles.
- Write out and act out your notes.
- Add movement as you learn.
- Before reading a chapter of a book, briefly preview it by looking at the illustrations, section headings, etc., and get a "feel" for it, act it out in your mind or physically feel what it would be like to be the various characters or to use the material presented.
- Use a standing desk (which is better for your back). Thomas Jefferson, Virginia Woolf and former U.S. Secretary of Defense Donald Rumsfeld used standing desks.
- Do a little pacing, where you will not disturb others, while you think.
- Take frequent breaks to get yourself and your thinking moving.

Auditory Digital

- Identify the key facts and figures. Given what you know, do they make sense? What is missing for you to understand this information? Get curious, ask questions. Dig deeper and explore what is behind this data.
- Notice how facts and figures can come together to make a compelling argument. If what someone says does not make sense, where does his train of thought break down?
- Before reading a chapter of a book, briefly preview it by looking at the illustrations, section headings, etc. Does this information make sense given what you already know or what has been described in the book so far? Given what you know, what is the next logical piece?

Another way to motivate your child

Author Bernice McCarthy noticed that children in her classes learned in different ways. They were motivated to explore the answers to one of four distinct questions: Why, What, How, and What if. She expanded these observations further and developed the 4MAT system (*The 4MAT System: Teaching to Learning Styles with Right/Left Mode Techniques*, Illinois, USA: Excel Incorporated, 1981). The 4MAT system provides a useful format for understanding how to motivate students and for writing essays or designing presentations. The four key components of the 4MAT system are:

- **Why** is this of interest? These students learn best by discussing the reasons why this subject is of interest or why they should do something. Until they get this "why" question answered, they are reluctant to take action or pay attention to the material. Motivate these learners by demonstrating how the material can be useful. About 35 percent of the U.S. population has this learning style.
- **What** is this? These students learn best when they get answers to the questions: What? When? Where? Who? In other words, they are looking for information – facts and figures – either orally or on a handout. About 22 percent have this learning style.
- **How** does this work or how do I use this? These students learn best by doing and being coached on how to do something. They want to get a feel for it, by participating in an exercise or being coached on doing it. They tend to ignore written manuals and just start using equipment, pushing buttons here and there to discover how the equipment works. They want a hands-on approach. This is the learning style for about 18 percent of the U.S. population.
- **What if?** These people learn best through self-discovery and want to explore future applications of what they're learning. They examine new ways to do

things to answer the question, "I wonder what would happen if I did things in a different way?" About 25 percent have this learning style.

In the 1970s, Bernice McCarthy also realized that most of the material presented in school was to answer only one of these questions – What? – with facts and figures. This is most likely still true today in many school systems.

As is the case with visual, auditory, kinesthetic and auditory digital, your children may prefer getting answers to one or two of the four questions. However, the student who will be most successful is the one who explores all four questions. You can assist your children:

- First, by discovering which of the four questions is of most interest to them and motivating them to learn by presenting material in this format.
- Then, by encouraging them to explore answers to the other questions. One way is to help them realize that having answers to the other questions provides greater understanding and makes the answers to their preferred question richer.

Developing an essay or class presentation
Your children will be asked to write an essay or give a presentation to their class. When asked to do so, they may draw a blank or not know how to get started or make it interesting for their audience.

The 4MAT system can help in this situation:

- Help your child decide on a topic and title. A title such as "How to write a good essay" is better than simply "Essays." Notice the former title generates curiosity – it answers the question "Why would I read this?" It indicates "what" is going to be covered, specifies "how" to do it, and the "what if" learner may be intrigued to explore what would happen if she did it this way.
- Generally, a good approach in structuring an essay or presentation is to have your child prepare an outline that answers the four questions in the order presented. She can begin by providing a one-sentence answer to the following four questions:
  o Why would someone be interested in this topic?
  o What will be covered – details, facts and figures?
  o How is it done? What is the process?
  o What if this process was followed or not followed? What would the consequences be?
- Now have your child expand her one-line answers into one or more paragraphs.
- Have her enrich her essay or presentation by helping people see, hear, feel and make sense of her topic.

8.7 EFFECTIVE LEARNING STRATEGIES

You and your children have strategies, habits and rituals for virtually everything you do. Some of these strategies work very well and others do not provide you with your desired results. A good strategy for music would have auditory as the main component, while kinesthetic is an important part of a strategy for learning dance or martial arts. And for storing and recalling information, visual is most often the critical piece – a picture is worth a thousand words. Here are some strategies that have proven to be very effective.

Spelling

Many people, both children and adults, have difficulty with spelling. It's not that they are poor spellers; it's that they are using an ineffective strategy.

Frequently, people who have difficulty spelling will move their eyes to kinesthetic (down to their right for right-handed people), often getting into feelings of embarrassment or hopelessness as they recall bad experiences associated with spelling at school or home. Others attempt to spell by sounding out the word phonetically. The problem is that in English, many words are not spelled the way they sound – for example, phonetics (fonetiks), one (won), eight (ate), know (no)."

Robert Dilts has studied good spellers (*Dynamic Learning*, Robert Dilts and Todd Epstein, Meta Publications, 1995) and discovered that a visual spelling strategy works best. The following is based on Dilts' work.

1. Have your child write the word on a piece of paper and break it into syllables (e.g., Albuquerque: al-bu-quer-que). Notice that we are using the concept of chunking; that is, breaking the word into smaller, more manageable chunks. This is similar to what we do with telephone numbers. In this way, we don't have to remember the whole word or telephone number, simply the first chunk. We spell and memorize that correctly, then the second chunk and so forth.
2. Have your child close his eyes and recall a time when he felt relaxed and confident.
3. Once he's fully into these feelings, have him open his eyes and place the paper with the correct spelling slightly above his eye level in visual remembered (for right-handed people, up to their left).
4. Have him look at the correct spelling and take a mental snapshot of it.
5. Remove the paper. While he maintains the correct spelling in his mind's eye and the relaxed, confident state, have your child say the word and then spell the word, one chunk at a time. If he experiences problems, return to step two.

6. While he still maintains the correct spelling in his mind's eye and the relaxed, confident state; have him spell the word backward, one chunk at a time. If he experiences problems, return to step two.

7. While he looks at the word in his mind's eye, have him say the word out loud, linking the image and sound together.

8. Ask him if he now feels confident and relaxed about successfully spelling the word.

The word is spelled backward for two reasons:

- This can only be done if your child is visually remembering the correct spelling.
- It provides proof to your child's conscious mind that he has indeed learned how to spell this word.

Additional ideas:

- Make it fun. You can encourage young children to challenge the other parent to see if she can spell the word forward and backward. Children enjoy doing something their parents can't.
- Have young children associate a picture with the word. If the word is *cat*, have your child visualize a cat with the word *cat* written on it.
- Encourage your children to repeat the exercise over a period of time to install in long-term memory.
- Use different colors for the chunks to make them standout.
- Have your children add a kinesthetic component by tracing the letters with their fingers.
- Avoid forcing your children to write out words they misspelled while in an unresourceful state.

Mathematics facts

Did you struggle memorizing the multiplication tables when you were in grade school? Turning it into a visual activity can make it easier. Prepare flash cards for all of the times tables, as illustrated in figure 14.

In a similar manner to the spelling strategy, encourage your children to relax and feel confident while snapping a mental picture of the flash card as it is held slightly above eye level in visual remembered. Have them see the picture of the flash card in their mind's eye, then tell you the following facts: $6 \times 8 = 48$, $8 \times 6 = 48$, $48 \div 8 = 6$ and $48 \div 6 = 8$. Notice that both multiplication and division are being handled at the same time. Assist your children with working their way through the other combinations, gradually picking up speed as they gain confidence. Replacing the multiplication and division symbols with plus and minus symbols provides a visual way to learn addition and subtraction.

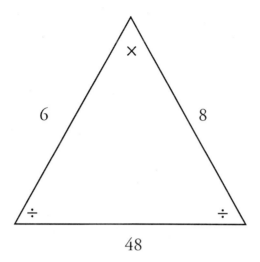

FIGURE 14: FLASH CARD FOR MULTIPLICATION AND DIVISION

Remembering stories

Do your children have difficulty remembering what they have read? Making pictures would help.

When children first start to read, the books are almost all pictures, with few words. As you or a teacher reads to your children, differing tones of voice and questions about feelings simultaneously connect the visual, auditory and kinesthetic senses (called a *synesthesia* in NLP) creating a stimulating and memorable experience. As your children advance in school, they read more by themselves and the number and size of the pictures decrease, while the number of words increases until they are faced with books primarily filled of words.

Those students who enjoy reading bring the words to life by creating pictures, sounds and feelings in their minds as they read. Other students mainly focus on sounding out the words, paying little attention to what they're reading.

To improve your children's enjoyment of reading and their ability to recall what they have read, encourage them to:

- Form an initial picture in their mind of what the book is about based on the book's title and chapter titles.
- Add more details and modify the picture, making it into a movie and connecting sounds and feelings to specific parts of the picture to create a richer experience, as each chapter is read.

8.8 VISUALIZATION

Visualization and mental rehearsal is using your mind to experience working through an activity to achieve an outcome. And it's more than simply seeing it in your mind – bring in sounds, feelings and if appropriate tastes and smells.

Does it work? There are many examples that show the power of visualization. Consider the following:

Australian psychologist Alan Richardson took three groups of basketball players and tested their ability to make free throws. The first group was instructed to spend twenty minutes a day practicing free throws. The second group was told not to practice, while the third group visualized shooting perfect baskets for twenty minutes a day. As expected, the second group showed no improvement. The first group improved 24 percent. Using simply the power of the mind, the third group improved 23 percent, almost as much as the group that practiced. (Mary Orser and Richard Zarro, *Changing Your Destiny*, Harper & Row, 1989, p.60). Note: the participants in this study already knew how to shoot free throws. Visualization did not teach them how to shoot free throws; it helped them improve their technique.

The process (illustrated with the basketball example above):

1. Make yourself comfortable. Relax and breathe deeply. You may choose to have some music playing softly in the background.
2. Identify your desired, clearly described, achievable outcome – successfully shooting free throws. Often this outcome is a part of a much larger outcome – in this case, being a good basketball player.
3. Close your eyes and create a picture in your mind in which you're about to shoot a free throw. Be fully associated (looking through your own eyes) and see what you see as you step to the free throw line with the basketball in your hand. Notice the feel of the basketball as you bounce it once or twice; hear the sound as the ball hits the floor and then your hand; hear what you're saying to yourself.
4. Take your shot, noticing what you feel, see and hear as you release the ball.
5. Hear the ball swish through the net and the crowd cheer and notice how you react and the feeling you get from successfully shooting the free throw.
6. Spend twenty to thirty minutes repeating this process, then again each day for a week.

Notes:

- For visualization to be successful: Involve as many senses as possible and adjust the qualities of the picture, sounds and feelings (submodalities – make the picture bigger, brighter, closer or the sounds louder or more rhythmic or the feelings more or less intense) to make this experience as real as possible.

• You are in first position for this exercise – looking through your own eyes and fully experiencing it from your perspective.

• If this activity involves the interaction with one or more other people (martial arts, giving a presentation to your class), during steps two and three you may wish to briefly view the experience from second or third position. By doing this you can assess the impact of your actions on others and how they may react, or you can give yourself some independent advice on how to improve.

• At the end of the visualization, notice how great you feel having achieved your outcome, and allow this feeling to move throughout your body.

• As with anything, practice makes perfect.

Visualization is a long-standing technique used by self-help experts and coaches to increase motivation, reduce anxiety, improve interpersonal interactions and improve performances (athletic and otherwise). The main reasons visualization enhances success and self-improvement are:

• Increases confidence – makes the outcome more real, more likely to occur.

• Improves motivation – as your dreams become more likely, you are more inclined to take action.

• Allows you to practice and test different ideas safely in a short period.

Many of us have used visualization in the past. However, often we have done it for something we truly didn't want to achieve; thus we visualizing ourselves failing.

Visualization has the same effect as physically doing the activity

When your children (or you) undertake a new activity, neural pathways are formed that allow them to repeat this activity again in the future. If the activity is discontinued, the neural pathways begin to decline and eventually disappear. On the other hand, if this activity is repeated regularly, the associated pathways become well-formed, signals flow easily and the activity becomes a way of life or habit. The brain can't tell the difference between when an action is physically taken or when that action is visualized. In either case, the neural pathways get activated and enhanced. This is an important concept that provides your children with a means to develop new habits and to significantly change how they live their lives. To have your children successfully use visualization to install a strategy or habit and instill it as a way of life, the key is to use and/or visualize the new strategy for five to thirty days.

8.9 ADDRESSING TEST ANXIETY

Test and performance anxiety is something that rears its head often with regard to learning. Some students who really know their material don't do well because of test anxiety. The problem occurs when there is too much focus on the anxiety and stories are invented of impending failure.

Presented in this book are many different techniques you can use to assist your child in addressing test anxiety. A few of these are:

- Make learning and studying a regular activity. Cramming at the last minute only makes things worse. If your children have been actively studying all along and performing well in class and on small tests, they'll feel more comfortable and ready for the big test.
- Access the relaxed, yet alert alpha brainwave state. This is the learning state and is also the state most useful for performing well on tests. In this state, your children use their peripheral vision rather than foveal vision. Foveal vision is about fight or flight. In a state of fight or flight, they may have difficulty remembering much more than their name. This is certainly not the state in which to write a test.
- Establish a resource anchor. Having a resource anchor that your children can fire off as they enter the room or pick up the test paper can put them in a resourceful, relaxed state.
- Add resources. The Dock of the Bay exercise is great for your children to add additional mental resources to feel good about themselves and do well on the test.
- Use submodalities. If your children are making pictures, sounds and feelings in their head about failing, have them adjust the visual, auditory and kinesthetic submodalities (e.g., make the picture smaller, darker, farther away). You can also use the swish pattern to assist your children in linking motivational pictures, sounds and feelings of success with taking a test.
- Use visualization. Have your children practice visualizing being knowledgeable and successful taking the test. Far too often, visualization is used unconsciously to reinforce and plant in their minds the potential of failing.
- Explore limiting beliefs. The Museum of Old Beliefs exercise can be used to assist your children with moving beyond beliefs that may have limited them in the past.

> We can learn something new
> any time we believe we can.
>
> — *Virginia Satir*

Providing a different interpretation

Anxiety is an emotion connected to your interpretation of some future event. If you change this to a neutral or positive interpretation, anxiety is not an option. That is reframe – a topic discussed earlier in this book.

You have energy moving through your body all the time. Sometimes it's more noticeable than other times. When you experience this energy, you're inclined to give it a label. Your children do the same. Whatever label you give it will influence your current and future behaviors. Labeling the energy moving through your body prior to a test or any activity you view with anticipation as anxiety predisposes you to the ensuing dysfunctional behaviors. What if it's not anxiety, but excitement or an eagerness to demonstrate how well you know the subject? Would this interpretation not serve you better?

In the case of children, far too often, they view tests as judgments about themselves – often judgments at an identity level. In their mind, they pile on all sorts of consequences if they don't perform well on the test. The vast majority of these consequences are fictitious. A test is simply a measurement of how much a person knows about a subject at a certain point in time. If you think about it, often there is a plan B or C that can be followed that will address the consequences and make up for rare underperformance on a test.

The following process will help your child in addressing anxiety over an upcoming test:

- Have your child determine the point in time when she knows she's done well on a test. For some people, they know immediately after writing the test. Others don't know until they receive the test score.
- Have her relax, close her eyes and imagine floating out of her body. In her mind's eye, have her see herself down below as she floats up and up. As she floats higher and higher, suggest to her that she floats out into the future to a time five minutes after she knows she's successfully completed the test.
- Given that she's successfully completed the test, how does she feel now? And the anxiety? It's gone because she is now enjoying the success of her labors.
- Have her really enjoy her success, feeling it going throughout her whole body, bathing each and every cell. Have her take these good feelings and float back to the present and then bring them fully into her body.
- Now have her think about the actual upcoming test and notice that she feels quite differently about it.

Laughing away anxiety

Laughter can have a positive impact on everyone's life:

- It boosts the immune system by increasing the amount of infection-fighting antibodies.
- It increases blood oxygen and exercises the cardiovascular system, which improves the coordination of brain functions such as enhancing alertness and memory.
- It allows the release of pent-up emotions – tension, stress, anxiety, anger, grief and depression.
- It makes us feel happy by boosting endorphin levels and decreases epinephrine levels, the body's stress hormone

Why not make laughter a regular part of your family's activity? What would happen if each evening a different family member was responsible for presenting one socially acceptable joke or cartoon? Would you and your family "lighten up," have more fun and contribute to your overall health?

Next time, a situation arises where your children may feel anxious, help them find something to laugh about.

Determining what's important

As a former university professor, I find that a number of students are not successful on tests because they simply do not know what's important – they can't see the forest for the trees.

You or your children may wish to have a conversation with their teachers to gain clarity on:

- The overall objectives of the course and how the teacher will know that students are making good progress.
- How this material is related to previously studied material.
- How this material forms a base for new material that will be covered later.

Use the precision model to gain clarity on these and other questions. Know what the teacher expects your children to know and have regularly scheduled times and habits to meet these objectives. When your children don't know what specifically to study, this can create a great deal of confusion, extra work and anxiety.

Breathing

People think they know how to breathe, yet far too often they hold their breath or breathe very shallowly. In a stressful situation, this only makes them feel more stressed.

Breathing deeply in a slow, rhythmic manner:[8]

- Acts as a mini meditation and can help you to relax and perform better mentally and physically.
- Helps your lungs and blood vessels function better.
- Helps improve the drainage of your lymphatic system, which removes toxins from your body.

The following exercise, which you can teach your children, will help you learn how to breathe in a slow, rhythmic manner:

1. Lie flat on the floor. Take a slow deep breath – about five seconds to fully inhale. Lying on the floor for the first couple of times you practice breathing will help you to fill your lungs naturally, rather than simply extending your chest.
2. When your lungs are totally full, exhale slowly, taking about seven seconds to let all the air out.
3. Repeat.

Getting in touch with nature

Next time you or your children are feeling stressed, get in touch with nature. Go for a walk or relax in a natural setting. If that isn't possible, look out the window at a nature scene.

In a recent experiment, ninety participants (thirty in three groups) in an office setting were exposed either to (a) a window with a view of a nature, (b) a high-definition plasma screen displaying the same nature scene outside the window, or (c) a blank wall. Results showed that in terms of heart rate recovery from low-level stress the participants with window seats recovered most quickly and the plasma was no more restorative than a blank wall ("A plasma display window? The shifting baseline problem in a technologically mediated natural world." Kahn, P. H., et al., *Journal of Environmental Psychology*, June 28, 2008, pp. 192–199).

Exercising

Recent research shows that middle school students who perform more vigorous physical activity than their more sedentary counterparts tend to do better in school. The researchers found that students taking a physical education course compared to those who did not take a physical education course did no better or worse in their academic classes. However, they did find that students who took part in more vigorous physical activities – such as soccer, football, swimming,

---

8. www.realage.com/agingcenter/articles.aspx?aid=10487, July 2009

running or skateboarding – did approximately 10 percent better in core classes such as math, science, English and social studies. The difference between vigorous activity and moderate activity is heart rate and breathing. Moderate activities such as walking or raking leaves don't get the heart rate up or make the person breathe harder ("Effect of physical education and activity levels on academic achievement in children," *Medicine & Science in Sports & Exercise*, August 2006, Vol. 38, No. 8, pp. 1515–1519).

Other research shows that exercising during the day can improve your productivity at work and make you feel more positive. Although the study involved employees, I'm convinced the results would be similar for students. The study found that employees who exercised before work or during lunch breaks were better able to handle the day's demands. Their general attitude also improved ("Exercising at work and self-reported work performance," J.C. Coulson, *International Journal of Workplace Health Management*, 2008, Vol. 1, No. 3, pp. 176–197):

• 72 percent reported improvements in time management on exercise days.
• 79 percent said mental and interpersonal performance was better.
• 74 percent said they managed their workload better.
• 41 percent felt more motivated to work.

8.10 PROVIDING FEEDBACK

Providing feedback, whether it is asked for or not, seems to be a regular feature of being a parent. You provide opinions to other family members in the hope that they will change their thoughts or behaviors in some way. Yet do they really hear what you're saying? Are you presenting your feedback in a way that they are open to receiving or at least considering?

I have chosen to include feedback in this chapter on Effective Learning because it seems parents often give feedback on their children's progress in school or with regard to learning. Although you may be well intentioned in providing your thoughts, sometimes it's not appropriate, or perhaps it's not received the way it was intended or appreciated. The problem is that the delivery mechanism used may not be the most appropriate.

There are many different approaches to providing feedback. At one end of the spectrum are those who never compliment you on what you have done well, only offering feedback when there is something that needs correcting. If you've been subject to this type of feedback, you know that after a while you begin tuning out these types of people and even avoid engaging them in any meaningful conversation. At the other end of the spectrum are those who sugar coat the feedback to such a degree that you're not really sure of the point they are trying to make.

So how can you provide feedback? I believe there needs to be some balance – let your children know what they're doing well and hence should do more of, and also let them know where there is room for improvement.

Feedback sandwich

A popular form of feedback is the *feedback sandwich*. Simply, what this means is you sandwich any feedback that may be interpreted in some way as negative between positive comments. When done appropriately, this can provide a nice balance between those things your children have done well and those areas where you believe your children could improve.

The feedback sandwich does have its drawbacks:

- Metaphorically, this approach is often viewed as a bun (the positive feedback) with meat (the negative or constructive feedback). This is unfortunate, as the "meat" of the matter may actually be about how the other person has done something particularly well. That is, the "meat" does not have to be negative.
- The positive feedback may be very thin and the recipient perceives this as a weakly veiled attempt to only criticize.
- The parent, either because she does not have confidence in what she wants to say or does not want to upset her children, may place too much emphasis on the positive feedback and provide little "meat" or direction for improvement.
- Knowing that the feedback will include both positive and negative points, your children may wonder if all the feedback is relevant. That is, were some valid points introduced or was unwarranted emphasis placed on one or more points simply to provide more of a balance?

Improving the feedback sandwich

The feedback sandwich is a good place to start, and the question should then be: How can we improve it?

Know the context
Sometimes, in your attempt to be helpful, you provide feedback without knowing the context or purpose of your children's actions.

For example, suppose your child brings home an abstract art picture he drew at school. You, not being a fan of abstract art, offer your opinion of his work without knowing that he drew it at the request of the teacher. In a case like this, determine the context before providing feedback.

You may wish to link your feedback to your child's stated outcome or values. If your child's outcome is to achieve an "A" in history, you may say to her, "Since your stated outcome is to get an "A" in history, I have some comments I believe will help you do that. Would you like to hear them?" Asking and receiving permission to provide feedback helps to ensure it's received the way it's intended.

Focus on improvement rather than criticism
Far too often, feedback comes across as criticism. Children exposed to criticism either rebel against it or become reluctant to take the initiative for fear of generating more criticism. To avoid your feedback being interpreted as criticism, identify the issue and desired outcome, praise your children for what they've accomplished so far, and explore whether they're open to suggestions to improve on what they're already doing well or to avoid potential difficulties.

Avoid getting caught up in the rules
We have rules for everything; sometimes they're written down and sometimes just assumed.

When you were growing up, you may have been subjected to a set of rules from your parents in a time and place quite different from that which your children are experiencing. Those rules may have been appropriate then and not so appropriate now.

There are always exceptions to the rules and sometimes the rules need to be changed. Before providing feedback, check to see if the rules really apply in this situation.

Use NLP's logical levels as a guide
NLP's logical levels can be used as a guide for presenting your feedback. You may choose to focus on:

- Environment – where, when and with whom. That is, your children may have chosen an inappropriate (or great) location, time or group of people.
- Behavior. What specifically did they do or not do?
- Strategies/Capabilities. You may wish to comment on their approach (strategy) or maybe a capability/skill they demonstrated or failed to demonstrate.
- Beliefs/Values. Unless your children have told you what they believe and value, it's difficult to provide feedback at the Beliefs/Values level. You can, however, ask questions about their beliefs and values and then provide feedback on this information.
- Identity. At this level, only positive praise is accepted. You're best advised to avoid any negative feedback using such words as *incompetent, lazy, stupid* or *bad*. This type of feedback can be devastating – it strikes right at the core of their existence and influences how they live the rest of their lives. Instead, comment on the *behaviors* that led you to this conclusion.
- Spirituality/Purpose. Here, you may wish to ask questions about the purpose of their actions and their connection to a larger system.

Speak what is true for you
Speak from your heart and talk about the impact of your children's actions on you. For example, "When you did *x*, I felt *y*." Your children can argue about the impact of their actions on others; however, they can't dispute the impact their actions had on you.

Be clear as to your purpose
When giving feedback, ask yourself, "For what purpose am I providing this feedback?" If it is to prove you know more than your children, to bring your children down a peg or two or it seems to be the thing to do, then maybe you should reconsider and explore what you can do to move yourself forward.

While sometimes your purpose is honorable and appropriate, your feedback may be focused on your children performing a specific behavior – one you may find easy to do, yet they may feel is too prescriptive or not feasible or not acceptable. In this situation, it may be more appropriate to raise the issue and then volunteer to work with your children to explore ways it can be addressed.

Ensure your children are open to receiving feedback
Before giving feedback, make sure you've been invited to do so or ask your children if they would appreciate receiving feedback. If the answer is no, move on to something else. Providing feedback when it is not asked for or appreciated is simply a waste of time. At best, it may satisfy a short-term need you have, yet it may not build a healthy, mutually supportive relationship with your children.

8.11 OVERVIEW OF THIS CHAPTER

FIGURE 15: MIND MAP OF THIS CHAPTER:
EFFECTIVE LEARNING

Index

About the Author:
Roger Ellerton, PhD, CMC

Roger is passionate about helping others get what they desire in life. As a longtime successful businessman, university professor, NLP trainer/coach, public speaker, author and parent, he has first-hand experience with the personal/professional balancing act required in these busy times. He is a former tenured faculty member at the University of New Brunswick, an executive in the Canadian federal government, a certified management consultant (CMC) and he has been listed in the *International Who's Who in Education*.

Roger believes that each of us can achieve the success we desire by developing our authentic selves, mastering internal and external congruence and taking charge of our lives. He is the safe, helpful person next door whom everyone should have access to. He is a certified NLP trainer and has been delivering NLP and personal growth seminars and coaching services since 1996. Participants often remark how much fun it is being in his classes, how clearly he presents the material and how ready and willing he is to answer their questions and provide insights they have long been searching for.

For over twenty years, Roger has been a student of personal development methodologies. He continues to transform his own life while assisting others from all walks of life and all ages to learn, to address challenges at work and at home and to get more of what they desire in life. He is the father of four, an avid gardener and nature lover and he enjoys lending a hand to others.

He is the author of two books: *Live Your Dreams Let Reality Catch Up: NLP and Common Sense for Coaches, Managers and You* and *Live Your Dreams Let Reality Catch Up: 5 Step Action Plan* and of over fifty articles on NLP. Roger received his BSc. and MSc. from Carleton University in Ottawa, Canada, and his PhD from Virginia Tech, Blacksburg, Virginia, USA.

Roger is the founder and managing partner of Renewal Technologies Inc. For more information on his seminars, coaching and consulting services, visit www.renewal.ca.